A GUIDE TO EXPLORING

OAK CREEK
AND THE
SEDONA AREA

A GUIDE TO EXPLORING

OAK CREEK
AND THE
SEDONA AREA

Stewart Aitchison

Drawings by Veruska Vagen
Maps by Richard Firmage

1989
RNM Press

Book Design by Richard Firmage
Front and back cover photographs by Stewart Aitchison
Front cover: Gambel Oak leaves in Bear Wallow Canyon
Back cover: Cathedral Rock and Courthouse Butte

Library of Congress Catalog Number 88-062649
ISBN: 0-9621511-0-6

Printed in the United States of America

Printed on acid-free paper which meets the minimum
requirements of the American National Standard for Permanence
of Paper for Printed Library Materials Z39.48-1984.

Published by RNM Press, a division of Peth-Saige, Inc.
Box 8531, Salt Lake City, Utah 84108

Distributed by Utah Geographic Books, Inc.,
Box 8325, Salt Lake City, Utah 84108 (801-583-2333)

DEDICATION

For my mother and father,
who brought me to the canyons

PREFACE

Ten years have passed since I wrote my first book about Oak Creek Canyon, a guide primarily for the hiker. During the ensuing years, my personal explorations and study of the Oak Creek area have continued. Discussions with various specialists in geology, archaeology, biology, and history have led me to new concepts and conclusions about the area's natural history.

The number of visitors to Oak Creek Canyon has more than doubled in the last decade from about 1.2 million people to more than 2.5 million. In 1986, at just one location, Slide Rock, the Forest Service recorded 275,000 visitors. Some 12,000 people now reside in the Oak Creek area.

U.S. Highway 89A through the canyon and State Highway 179 south of Sedona have both been designated as State Scenic Roads. An area in the canyon adjacent to Slide Rock and a portion of lower Oak Creek are being developed into state parks. Coconino County has designated the canyon from Pumphouse Wash to Midgley Bridge as a "Special Resource Area." Prior to 1984 when Congress designated two backcountry areas as wilderness—the Red Rock-Secret Mountain Wilderness and the Munds Mountain Wilderness—much of the area had been considered as a possible national monument. The scenic and natural resources of the area are now recognized as something worthy of our careful stewardship.

The Red Rock Country's natural history has continued to evolve as well. New animal and plant sightings have been recorded, the rocks have received more attention from geologists, and new ideas about the region's geologic history have been formulated. Just as nature deposits sediment and later strips it away through erosion, scientists' theories are set down, tested by time and research, and sometimes reworked or abandoned entirely in favor of other ideas and conclusions.

In preparation for writing this completely new guide, I have re-hiked the trails, driven all the roads and jeep trails, scoured the literature, and talked at length with many experts to glean the latest information. I have endeavored to present a brief summary of the most current understanding of the natural and human history of Oak Creek Canyon. But unanswered questions remain.

In a popular work such as this, I do not want to overwhelm the reader with too much information. On the other hand, neither do I want to lead the reader astray by summarizing too much. The "Further Reading" section will guide the curious to more detailed discussions.

While this guide is primarily designed to serve visitors who are passing through in motor vehicles, if that is you, I hope you will take time to get out of your vehicle and take at least a few short walks. You need to feel the rock under your feet and to smell the pine-scented air along the rim to experience Oak Creek. To this end, trailhead locations are given in tables to help you.

As I write this preface in the cool, damp shade beside Oak Creek, occasionally gazing into a swirling reflection of a golden cliff, I wonder about the changes that will occur here in the next decade. More people will undoubtedly come to see and enjoy the beauty of this place. The dynamic ecosystem of the canyon and of the Red Rock Country will continue to evolve—its course dictated by the environment which in turn is modified directly and indirectly by the presence of man. Federal, state, county and local governments face a significant challenge in managing the natural resources of this area. All of us share in this responsibility; special land management designations alone will not preserve the values we seek here. Oak Creek Canyon and the Red Rock Country is a very special place and it merits our special care.

It is my hope that ten years from now this little book will still be regarded as a capsule natural history of a remarkable area and not an epitaph of something that once was.

ACKNOWLEDGMENTS

I am not alone in my love for the Red Rock Country. There are many scientists, land managers, amateur naturalists, photographers, residents and visitors studying and exploring the area. I have had the good fortune to learn from them.

The Coconino National Forest personnel went beyond the call of duty to assist me in this project. I would like to thank in particular Loyd Barnett, Bob Gilles, Greg Goodwin, John Nelson, Peter Pilles, and Ron Plapp.

I also wish to thank John Schreiber, manager of Red Rock State Park, John Boeck, manager of Slide Rock State Park, and Cheryl Steenerson, Arizona Parks Operation Coordinator; Northern Arizona University geologists Ron Blakey, Richard Holm and NAU biologist Dean Blinn; Museum of Northern Arizona botanists Art Phillips and Barbara Phillips; Arizona Game and Fish Department biologists James Landye and Scott Reger; entomologist Milton Sanderson; geologist Wayne Ranney; pilot Bruce Grubbs; Flagstaff Public Librarian John Irwin; NAU Special Collections Librarian William Mullane; Northern Arizona Audubon Society members Virginia Gilmore and Alma Greene; Sedona Westerner Robert Freeman; and Martha Blue.

Photographers Chuck Bame, Gene Balzer, Tom Bean, Martos Hoffman, and Brian Street kindly submitted stunning pictures for consideration.

Rick Reese and Linda Oswald of the Utah Geographic Series and book designer Richard Firmage deserve the credit for transforming my rough ideas into a finished book. A special thanks goes to Veruska Vagen for producing the lovely pen and ink drawings.

Grateful acknowledgment is made to Zane Grey, Inc. for permission to quote from *The Call of the Canyon* by Zane Grey.

We are all indebted to those dedicated men and women who have the difficult task of managing our public lands.

I would like to hear from you. Please send comments, suggestions or corrections to the author in care of Utah Geographic Series, P.O. Box 8325, Salt Lake City, UT 84108. Thanks for your help.

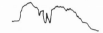

CONTENTS

A GUIDE TO EXPLORING

OAK CREEK
AND THE
SEDONA AREA

INTRODUCTION

Oak Creek Canyon and the Red Rock Country of central Arizona is one of the world's loveliest places. Red buttes and cliffs tower over a clear, tumbling brook. Dark green forests mantle the higher rims while a profusion of broad-leafed trees and shrubs hug the stream. A myriad of birds, mammals, reptiles and amphibians make their homes in Oak Creek Canyon and the surrounding valleys and mesas. This is an area notable not only for its natural beauty but for the artistic and relaxed lifestyle of its human inhabitants.

After an exhilarating morning of birding, swimming, or sightseeing, numerous shops, galleries and restaurants invite the visitor and resident alike. Late afternoon brings out photographers who try to capture the last glow on the red rock. The energetic may take a hike along one of the many Forest Service trails in the area or strike out into the wilderness backcountry. Fishermen steal away to a favorite "hole" and kids of all ages splash and sun at slippery Slide Rock.

For the purposes of this book, the Red Rock Country has been divided into three major areas:

1) the main Oak Creek Canyon from its head at the switchbacks on U.S. Highway 89A downstream to its mouth at Sedona;

2) the complex of secret canyons and interspersed mesas northwest of Sedona and extending to the Sycamore Canyon Wilderness; and

3) the red rock country south and east of Sedona toward Interstate 17.

Come, explore with me this land of rock, stream, and dreams.

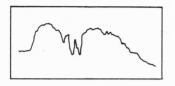

═══════PART I═══════
Road and Trail Guide

GENERAL OAK CREEK AREA MAP

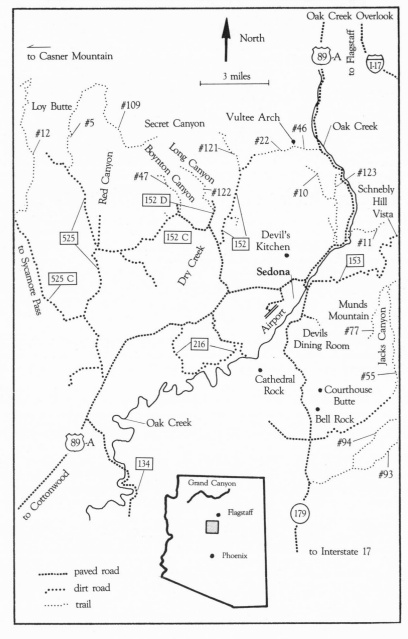

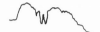

CHAPTER 1

THE CANYON

The very forest-fringed earth seemed to have opened into a deep abyss, ribbed by red rock walls and choked by steep mats of green timber. . . .At one point it appeared narrow and ended in a box. In the other direction, it widened and deepened, and stretched farther on between tremendous walls of red, and split its winding floor of green with glimpses of a gleaming creek, boulder-strewn and ridged by white rapids. . . .What a wild, lonely, terrible place. . . .This insulated rift in the crust of the earth was a gigantic burrow for beasts, perhaps for outlawed men—not for a civilized person. . . .

Zane Grey, *The Call of the Canyon*, 1921

The main Oak Creek Canyon can be conveniently broken into three approximately equal sections: upper, middle, and lower canyon. The description that follows is from north to south, but highway milepost figures are given in parentheses so the reader will be able to find his location whether driving from Sedona or from Flagstaff. The accompanying maps will aid in finding the areas under discussion and the Natural History Stops (eight in all) that are set forth below.

Drive slowly through the canyon on a late summer evening, and be prepared to brake for a striped skunk, spotted skunk, ringtail cat, gray fox, or even a mountain lion. Or, with binoculars in hand, spend an early morning in June wandering along the bank of the creek looking for birds; even a beginning birder should find more than a dozen species. The variety of life in the Oak Creek Canyon area is astounding. There are more than twenty kinds of fish, forty species of reptiles and amphibians, about 180 recorded species of birds, and nearly five dozen types of mammals. Add to these the insects, spiders and other invertebrates plus some 600 flowering plants, and you begin to get an appreciation for the biological wealth of the Red Rock Country.

Even to the casual observer, the plants and animals of Oak Creek are not scattered at random; they occur in recognizable groups or communities. What controls their distribution?

Temperature and precipitation are the most crucial environmental factors influencing the makeup of natural communities. These two factors are related to the basic weather patterns of the region and the influence of topography: the higher you go, the cooler and wetter; slopes facing the sun will be hotter and drier than slopes that are shaded.

Eight major plant communities have been described for the Oak Creek area. Going from wetter, cooler conditions to hotter, more arid conditions, they are: (1) Ponderosa Pine-Fir Forest, (2) Pinyon Pine-Juniper

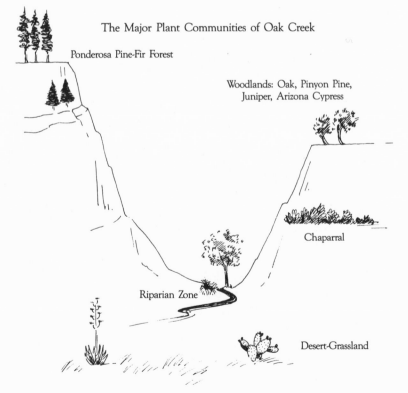

The Major Plant Communities of Oak Creek

Ponderosa Pine-Fir Forest

Woodlands: Oak, Pinyon Pine, Juniper, Arizona Cypress

Chaparral

Riparian Zone

Desert-Grassland

Woodland, (3) Evergreen Oak Woodland, (4) Arizona Cypress Woodland, (5) Chaparral, and (6) Desert Grassland. Along the creek, the riparian vegetation has been broken into the (7) Upper and (8) Lower Riparian Zones. The Upper Riparian has a predominance of coniferous species whereas the Lower Riparian contains mostly broad-leafed plants.

In many parts of the canyon these communities do not change abruptly from one to another. Rather, there is a blending or overlapping. These transition "ecotones" are often the areas with the greatest variety of animal life.

Animal communities are superimposed on the plant communities. Animals are more mobile than plants and may therefore range over several of the plant communities. Additionally, many animals migrate seasonally—some leaving the region entirely, others simply moving to a different elevation.

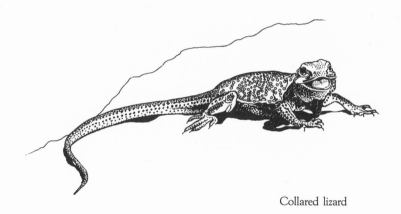

Collared lizard

UPPER OAK CREEK CANYON MAP

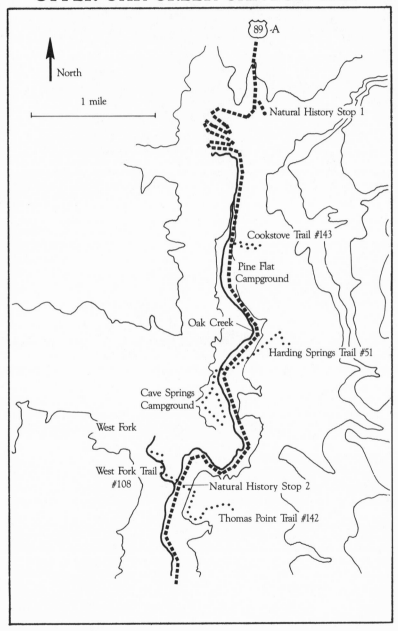

THE UPPER CANYON

The Mogollon Rim to West Fork

Driving south from Flagstaff on U.S. Highway 89A, there is little hint that the ponderosa pine forest is going to end abruptly on the brink of the Mogollon Rim. As you travel through the forest, notice the tall, orange-barked mature pines, their distinctive color indicating an age in excess of 200 years. Interspersed with the pines are small stands of Gambel oak, the only deciduous oak in Arizona. Some of the ponderosas occur in "dog-hair" thickets of small-diametered, crowded trees, an unfortunate result of over-controlling natural fires that have historically thinned such stands.

If you are on the road early in the morning or at dusk, beware of elk or mule deer that may be wandering along the shoulder. During the day, bright blue Steller's jays or an occasional Abert's squirrel with its tufted ears may be spotted. Fall travelers may also be treated to the sight of the annual "migration" of male tarantula spiders crossing the road while hunting for mates.

A sign warns to reduce speed, another illustrates a 7% grade ahead; you round a curve and suddenly the forest parts and a glorious rent in the Earth's crust is before you. Unlike the Grand Canyon that stupifies the senses with awe at its immense grandeur, Oak Creek is of a more manageable scale, intimate rather than intimidating, a place that beckons you welcome. Sinuous switchbacks lead down into a verdant sanctuary of forest, woodland and stream.

Stop at the Overlook (MP 390) to view the canyon at Natural History Stop 1.

Abert's squirrel

Natural History Stop 1
OAK CREEK OVERLOOK

Elevation: 6413 feet   Milepost 390, 15 miles north of Sedona

Here at the very head of the canyon is perhaps your first look into the " . . . wild, lonely, terrible place!" described by the heroine in Zane Grey's *Call of the Canyon*. It is not wild or lonely anymore, at least not in the main canyon, but a short walk from the road and you can find peace and undisturbed nature.

Oak Creek Canyon is fourteen miles long, averages about a mile and a half in width, and varies in depth from 1000 feet near its head to 2500 feet at its mouth. Notice that the west canyon rim (that's the one to your right) is more than 500 feet higher than the east rim. This difference is due to movement along the Oak Creek Fault. The fault is a major break in the Mogollon Rim, a 200-mile long escarpment cutting across Arizona and into New Mexico. In the far distance you can see the flat-topped summit of Wilson Mountain near the town of Sedona.

Note the differences in vegetation on the various slopes. Before you is a remarkable mosaic of coniferous forest blended with chaparral and even desert species. Far below, Oak Creek supports a lush ribbon of riparian or streamside species. On the south-facing slope directly below you are plants that have adapted to hot, arid conditions. The species include chapparal such as shrub live oak, manzanita, mountain mahogany and silk-tassel bush. The chaparral or

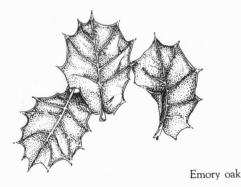

Emory oak

brush-thicket community continues southward along dry, rocky slopes and makes up the largest vegetational association of the canyon.

In the upper canyon, on the west, east, and north-facing slopes are ponderosa pine, Douglas fir, white fir, a few alpine firs, and Engelmann spruce. These plants are indicative of wetter, cooler conditions. A thousand feet below, Oak Creek issues out of fractures in the Coconino Sandstone and begins its thirty-mile journey to the Verde River. In the autumn, you may see clumps of scarlet red or bright yellow in the shady clefts of the cliffs. These are bigtooth maples and quaking aspen living in the micro-habitat provided by the cracks. Vermilion leaves along the road are most likely scarlet sumac.

From this point you can also see most of the different layers of rock that make up Oak Creek Canyon. Much of the rim, especially the east rim, is composed of dark gray basalt lava flows. Beneath the lava is the buff-white Kaibab Limestone slope followed by the massive, buff-colored Coconino Sandstone cliffs. Below the Coconino and blending into it is the reddish Schnebly Hill Formation; more about this layer later. The geology sign on the rim is outdated and lists Supai instead of the Schnebly Hill Formation.

Look again at the Coconino Sandstone cliff. About half-way down, the cliff-face is interrupted by a small slope or shelf where trees are often growing. At one time that portion of the cliff from the shelf up to the Kaibab was considered a separate layer. Here in Oak Creek it is an eolian or wind-blown deposit and considered part of the Coconino Sandstone. In other places, such as the Grand Canyon where it appears as a marine limestone/sandstone, that upper unit of rock is distinctive enough to have its own name, Toroweap.

Look to where the road swings around a "detached" hill on its journey to the canyon bottom. This hill and similar ones down the canyon are enormous chunks of the west wall that have become detached due to faulting.

While studying the geology, you may hear the "yank-yank" of a white-breasted nuthatch, the laughter of a group of white-throated swifts, or the swoosh of a violet-green swallow as it flies past the cliff's edge. As you walk back to your car, notice that in addition to the tall pines the flora includes mountain mahogany, Rocky Mountain juniper, red-barked manzanita, shrub live oak, and alligator juniper. In summer, lupine, bluebells, phlox, senecio, claret-cup

Lupine

hedgehog cactus, larkspur, fleabane, and other wildflowers bloom on the forest floor. This biologically diverse rim country is composed of a mixture of chaparral and forest plant species and contains animals typical of both habitats.

Take a moment to look northeast into Pumphouse Wash. This deep, narrow canyon offers several lessons in geology. The rim is composed of basaltic lava flows; you are probably standing on gray basalt. Between flows, there is often a "baked-soil" layer in which minerals, notably iron, have been oxidized red. These reddish-orange layers are particularly easy to see along the highway switchbacks.

Some of the lava flows formed vertical columns as the lava cooled, shrank, and fractured—a process called "columnar jointing." The famous Devil's Post Pile in Wyoming is a large- scale version of this same type of columnar jointing. Notice, too, that while the main Oak Creek Canyon seems fairly straight, Pumphouse is very crooked. The former's shape was predetermined by the fairly straight Oak Creek fault, whereas the latter canyon's zig-zag pattern is controlled by joints. More about joints can be found in Natural History Stop 2.

As you drive down the switchbacks, you are traveling back through geologic time. The lava flows, which at five to eight million years of age are relatively young, rest atop sedimentary rocks that were deposited in a warm, shallow sea about 250 million years ago. This Kaibab Limestone in turn overlies the Coconino Sandstone, an eolian or wind-blown dune deposit another twenty million years older. In several places where the highway crosses a fault, the sandstone has been crushed to powder by movement along the fracture. (See "Origin of the Rocks" on page 83 for a description of geologic strata in the canyon.)

At the base of the switchbacks you pass the **Sterling Springs Fish Hatchery** (MP 388) at the head of Oak Creek. A few more tenths of a mile and the road crosses the **Pumphouse Wash Bridge** (MP 387.7). The wash (here at its mouth actually a spectacular canyon) received its name from the fact that water used to be pumped from here to the lumber railroad near Flagstaff.

Fishermen try their luck for trout in the sparkling creek. Gila trout, now absent from the canyon, suffered from the introduction of other species. By 1898, rainbow trout, a fish not native to the Colorado River Basin or Oak Creek, were being planted. By 1913, hybrids of the two trout were present and shortly thereafter no more pure Gilas were caught.

Another native, the Gila mountain-sucker, is often seen feeding on algae, scraping it off the rocks with its cartilage-sheathed jaws. This fish is rarely eaten.

Gila Mountain-sucker

Some 55,000 rainbow and 20,000 brown trout are planted here annually. The stocked rainbows average a catchable nine inches in length and are released weekly from April through September. The browns are stocked as three-inch fingerlings in the fall. Special wild strains of rainbow and cutthroat trout are being raised at the Sterling Fish Hatchery and are occasionally planted in the creek. Apache trout, endemic to the White Mountains of Arizona, were introduced into Oak Creek in the past and a few may still exist.

While you are casting for that prize trout, notice the little cylinder-shaped objects on the creek bottom, no more than an inch in length and made of grains of sand and bits of twigs or leaves. Did you see them move? They are caddis fly larvae that build a hard case around their soft body for protection from trout and other predators. Oak Creek is home to three rare caddis fly species (*Apatania arizona*, *Rioptila arizonica*, and *Ithytrichia* which does not yet have a specific name). The checklist of fish in upper Oak Creek includes:

Rainbow Trout (Stocked)
Brown Trout (S)
Cutthroat Trout (Exotic)
Arizona Trout (E)
Gila Trout (Native) known only from historic records
Arctic Grayling (E)
Speckled Dace (N)
Gila Mountain-sucker (N)
Green Sunfish (E)
Bluegill (E)
Smallmouth Bass (E)

About a half mile beyond the bridge there is a large talus slope of gray boulders on the west wall (to your right as you drive down the canyon). Geologically speaking, this slope is actively pushing the creek farther east, which in turn is undermining the highway. A wonderful example of geology in action!

Here under the shade of giant white firs, Douglas firs, and ponderosa pines, roadside summer wildflowers include scarlet gilia, yellow evening-primrose, lupine, geranium, goldenrod, and fleabane.

You soon come to the popular **Pine Flat Campground** (MP 386.8). Next to the road at the north end of the campground is a large stone structure with pure spring water running out of a pipe. Opposite the spring

Evening-primrose

is the **Cookstove Trail**; it climbs 800 feet to the east rim in just over a half mile. It is possible to travel along the rim about a mile south and then descend back into the canyon on the **Harding Springs Trail**. This is a good trip to see the upper canyon and to experience the ecotone or transition between the coniferous forest and chaparral habitats. It is not unusual to see bracken fern, a moist forest denizen, living next to a species such as banana yucca that has adapted to arid conditions.

Continuing down the road another mile, you will notice an old orchard on your right, one of many within the canyon. Oak Creek is locally famous for its fruit, especially apples.

Just beyond the orchard is a sign for Troutdale and **Cave Springs Campground** (MP 385.9). The campground usually opens sometime in late May and is busy all summer. At the north end of the campground is a small cave where a spring has been developed for the campers. In 1912, Jess Purtyman used the cave as a kitchen and living quarters. Along the cave's walls are old inscriptions and unfortunately a great number of recent scratchings. Please do not deface the rock.

The upper portion of Oak Creek offers some fine birding. Birds are marvelous creatures—tiny bundles of energy wrapped in feathers. I imagine that they are often singing a melodious message of "Keep out. No trespassing!" This may work against other males of the same species but, alas, humans are not so affected.

The annual "migration" of campers into Oak Creek Canyon each spring and summer concerns biologists because of the human impact upon wildlife. One study examined the effect that campers are having on the birds in the Cave Springs Campground. After the campground was opened

Lesser Goldfinch

in late May, the number of breeding birds living within the campground decreased by forty percent.

Much of this loss can be attributed to direct human interference at nest sites. Maintenance of the campground inadvertently destroyed some nests; campers destroyed nests through the illegal removal of branches (probably for firewood); and some birds, notably warblers, solitary vireos, broad-tailed hummingbirds, and hairy woodpeckers, simply abandoned their nests. A few species such as Steller's jays and ravens did not leave the area as they seem to adapt easily to humans by feeding on food scraps.

The study continued over a number of breeding seasons and it was discovered that the kinds of birds composing the breeding population varied slightly from year to year. When spring came early, for example, summer tanagers nested in the upper canyon at Cave Springs Campground. The next year, winter would not loosen its grip on the high country and hepatic tanagers nested here. The following season was one of those "typical" springs in which, just as it seemed it was time for shorts and sunscreen, another winter storm would blow through. Amazingly, both hepatics and summer tanagers raised families in the area. (See partial list of breeding birds in the area on page 96.)

Opposite the entrance to Cave Springs Campground, a Forest Service sign marks the **Harding Springs Trail**. The springs are not on the trail but are located about a half mile north of the trailhead along the creek.

Another mile or so brings you to a Forest Service day-use area (MP 384.7), a pleasant bend in the creek and an abandoned orchard—a great place for a picnic and some bird watching. This is the site of the former Call of the Canyon Lodge. The three- story Lolomai Lodge once stood across the creek. As local legend has it, Zane Grey wrote his novel *The Call of the Canyon* here. (According to several of Grey's biographers, however, he actually started writing that novel at his home in Avalon, Catalina Island and finished it in Oregon.) The tale *The Call of the Canyon* was serialized in various issues of the *Ladies Home Journal* in 1921-1922, and was not published in book form until 1924. In 1923, Paramount Studios filmed a movie version of the novel within the canyon and in Flagstaff at the Santa Fe Railroad Station and the Weatherford Hotel. A heavy downpour delayed production, but allowed inclusion of a flash flood scene.

About a quarter of a mile farther down the road (384.5), a massive Coconino Sandstone wall marks the mouth of the **West Fork** of Oak Creek. There are a number of private residences here but wide shoulders provide a place to pull off and park. (Take care not to block anyone's driveway.) One driveway on the right side is chained-off but marked with Forest Service signs. Walk down this paved path to the creek to reach West Fork for Natural History Stop 2 and the West Fork Trail.

Natural History Stop 2

WEST FORK

Elevation: 5280 feet   Milepost 384.5

Walk down the blocked-off road (marked as West Fork Trail #108) past the blackberry bushes, scarlet sumac, wild grape, the tall white fir on your left, the Douglas fir on your right, around the bend where an old Arizona sycamore shades the path, and down to the creek. There used to be a bridge here, but it was destroyed in a flash flood a few years ago. Provided that the creek isn't flooding, cross on the stepping stones to reach the mouth of West Fork. Most of the boulders in the creek are made of more resistant basalt. The softer sedimentary rocks are quickly broken apart by running water.

The ruins of the old Mayhew Lodge are directly across the creek but they are fairly well hidden by the non-native trees-of-heaven.

Scarlet Gilia

Along this part of Oak Creek and the permanent stream of West Fork grow Arizona alder, box elder, narrowleaf cottonwood, bigtooth maple, velvet ash, Douglas fir, white fir, Arizona walnut, and Gambel oak. Shrubs include arroyo willow, red willow, scarlet sumac, and red osier dogwood. River sedge, horsetail rush, and watercress are common. Under the shady protection of the forest and cliff, poison ivy, wild grape, bracken fern, Arizona rose, Virginia creeper, bee balm, yellow monkeyflower, meadowrue, geranium, aster, columbine, cardinal flower, and lupine flourish.

West Fork was designated an Oak Creek Research Natural Area in 1931 and now lies within the 43,950-acre Red Rock-Secret Mountain Wilderness Area. Research Natural Areas protect unique vegetation types along with their wildlife and serve as benchmarks to monitor changes in the environment. Since it is a protected area, no camping or campfires are allowed in the first six miles of West Fork.

A number of relict species—plants or animals that had a wider distribution in the past, such as hophornbeam and the narrow-headed gartersnake—can be found in this area. It is also possible to see the Canyon's three species of tree squirrels in this locale. The Abert's squirrel is closely tied to ponderosa pine forest, the red squirrel is usually associated with spruce and fir, and the Arizona gray squirrel likes to feed on walnuts, acorns, juniper berries, and hackberries. The three plant communities are usually geographically separated, but here at West Fork all three are mixed together, thus all three species of squirrel also occur here.

Arizona gray squirrel

Where the trail first crosses West Fork, spend a moment taking in the grandeur of the scene. The descending notes of a hidden canyon wren will probably drift down to greet you.

The towering canyon walls are composed mainly of the massive, crossbedded Coconino Sandstone. The crossbedding or angled lines on the cliff surface represent bedding planes. Millions of years ago, wind drifted sand into huge dunes. The prevailing winds tended to deposit the sand layer by layer. Through time, as the prevailing wind direction changed, the layers of sand would be deposited at different angles. Eventually the bedding planes were preserved as the sand grains became cemented together to form sandstone.

The reddish cliff at creek level is composed of the upper part of the Schnebly Hill Formation. Oxidized particles of iron give this rock unit its color. The black stains running down the cliff face like paint spills are called desert varnish. This is an iron and manganese oxide stain or crust. How the varnish forms is not completely understood but it appears to be related to wet surfaces (such as where water runs down the cliff during storms) where dust containing the necessary minerals may stick. Some geologists believe a specialized bacteria living on the rock surface is the mechanism by which the mineral stain becomes fixed to the rock.

Along West Fork, water can often be seen seeping out of the rock walls. Ground water moving down through the sandstone apparently hits an impervious layer and begins to travel horizontally. When the moisture reaches a cliff face, it seeps out as a spring. The cement holding the grains of sandstone together can dissolve and lead to weakening of the rock. The weakened rock falls away and eventually a little recess or overhang may be formed.

You may have noticed here, and especially upstream near the day-use area, that the sandstone wall is broken by numerous vertical fractures called joints. Joints differ from faults in that there has been no appreciable movement of the rock on either side of the break. Joints sometimes form as overlying rock is removed through erosion and the underlying layers can "stretch with relief" from the tremendous weight. Uplifting can also generate jointing as well as faulting.

Joints tend to form at right angles to each other, and if widened by erosion into a canyon, the resulting gorge will zig and zag. West Fork and Pumphouse Wash are good examples of joint-controlled canyons. Oak Creek Canyon, on the other hand, follows a major fault, a relatively straight break.

Most visitors hurry down to West Fork without noticing the old **Thomas Point Trail** that ascends the east wall opposite the parking area. This route was pioneered by Jesse Jefferson Howard who built a cabin at the mouth of West Fork in 1870. Howard was the first Anglo settler in upper Oak Creek Canyon. He killed a sheepherder in California and served a short sentence at San Quentin Prison. He later came to Arizona and changed his name to Charley Smith Howard, but his hunting prowess and the grizzly steaks he served earned him the sobriquet "Bear" Howard. Twice during the 1870s, his daughter and her three children rode mules all the way from California to visit him. During one of these visits, Bear Howard had to go to Flagstaff (a three-day trip) for supplies. As he was riding down the trail into Oak Creek, he encountered a band of Apaches who were holding his daughter and grandchildren captive. Howard claimed to have killed seven of the Indians and rescued his family. In

1899, three days short of his ninety-fourth birthday, the great bear hunter turned conservationist died with an orphaned bear cub nestled at his feet.

Earlier, in 1887, John Thomas bought Howard's cabin and turned the property over to his son, Lou, who built a two-story log addition and opened the structure as a hunting and fishing lodge in 1895. Lou died in 1920 and his heirs sold the lodge to Jim Lamport, a civil engineer from Williams. Lamport's son and daughter-in-law operated the resort under the name "Tioga" until they sold it to Carl Mayhew in 1925.

The silent film, "Call of the Canyon," based on Zane Grey's novel, which was set in this location, was shot near the lodge in 1923. During the 1930s and 40s, Mayhew's Oak Creek Lodge, with just ten guest rooms, became a famous hideaway for movie stars, politicians, and writers, including Lord Halifax, President Herbert Hoover, Clark Gable, Susan Hayward, Caesar Romero, Jimmy Stewart, and Maureen O'Hara. Mayhew died at the lodge in 1943. In 1968 the Forest Service acquired the property through a land exchange and listed the site in the Register of National Historic Places. The Forest Service hoped the building would be restored and opened to the public, but, in 1980, before these plans could be realized, a transient's fire burned the lodge to the ground.

Indian paintbrush/Castilleja

MID OAK CREEK CANYON MAP

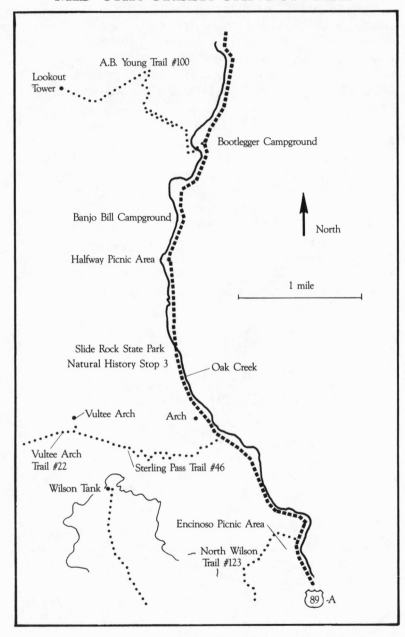

A.B. Young Trail #100

Lookout Tower •

Bootlegger Campground

North

Banjo Bill Campground

Halfway Picnic Area

1 mile

Slide Rock State Park
Natural History Stop 3

Oak Creek

Vultee Arch

Arch

Vultee Arch
Trail #22

Sterling Pass Trail #46

Wilson Tank

Encinoso Picnic Area

North Wilson
Trail #123

89 -A

□

MID-CANYON

West Fork to Indian Gardens

□

From West Fork (MP 384.5) down to Indian Gardens (MP 378.2), the canyon begins to widen a little. The scrubby chaparral on the canyon walls denotes drier conditions and the trees along the creek change from conifers to deciduous broad-leaf types. Several species of evergreen oaks also appear here.

During the late 1800s and early 1900s, pioneers homesteaded along the canyon floor. One reason for settling along the creek was to grow fruit and vegetables for sale in Flagstaff which is several thousand feet higher than the canyon bottom, has a much shorter growing season and has no permanent streams.

The canyon settlers built trails to the rim to shorten the travel distance to Flagstaff. Wagons were usually kept on top and only the draft animals were brought down the trail.

Bootlegger, Banjo Bill, and Manzanita are Forest Service campgrounds in the mid-canyon area that are open during the summer. Two picnic areas, Half-way and Encinoso, are also located here.

About 1.5 miles downstream from West Fork, across the creek from **Bootlegger Campground** (MP 383.1), the A.B. Young or **East Pocket Trail** takes off. This trail was originally built to take cattle up to the rim country. Today you may follow it for 2.4 miles and 2000 vertical feet to the East Pocket fire Lookout and a wonderful 360-degree view of the Canyon, the San Francisco Peaks, and the Verde Valley. A small portion of the Moenkopi Formation is exposed near the point where the trail reaches the rim.

There are several volcanic dikes between the Bootlegger Campground and the **Junipine Resort** (MP 382.9) One can be seen immediately north of the resort on the east side of the highway at road level. This vertical, dark-gray band of basalt illustrates the manner in which hot magma reached the surface to form a lava flow. There are several other dikes in this area, now exposed because of the cutting of the canyon.

A couple of miles farther south you arrive at **Slide Rock State Park** (MP 381.2), one of the most popular parts of the canyon. This is Natural History Stop 3.

Natural History Stop 3
SLIDE ROCK STATE PARK

Elevation: 4924 feet   Milepost 381.2

In 1926 Frank L. Pendley built the brown, two-story cabin that stands at the entrance to the State Park. This house was used as living quarters for his farm employees. Pendley tried to hire only men with families so that there would be enough local children to keep the school across the creek open.

He also constructed an irrigation ditch to bring water to his apple orchard. The "Pendley Ditch" is still in use today. The little houses facing the highway were built as tourist cabins.

After Pendley's death in the mid-1930s, his son, Tom, continued to produce apples, other fruit and corn to sell at a roadside stand. In late 1984 the land was acquired by the Arizona Parklands Foundation and in July, 1985, the State of Arizona purchased the property. The park was dedicated in October, 1987. During the next few years, the park will be developed to provide the visitor with information on the natural and cultural history of the area.

The fruit orchard is being maintained and is a good place to observe Arizona gray squirrels eating apples or yellow-bellied sapsuckers drilling neat rows of holes on the tree trunks. A small herd of Coues white-tailed deer frequent the park.

Harris' antelope squirrel

In the meantime, the park is open daily to the public for a nominal fee. No overnight camping is permitted. There are good spots for wading and sunning along the creek (which is national forest land that is jointly managed by the state and Forest Service). There is also the famous Slide Rock, a stretch of slippery creek bottom where, if the spirit and derriere are willing, you can slide down a slick chute.

From the parking area look carefully to the southwest and you will notice a splendid natural arch. The majority of natural arches in the Red Rock Country have formed where joints have been widened by erosion to leave behind a wall or fin of rock. Continued weathering on both sides of the fin make it thinner and thinner until a hole breaks completely through. The common arch- shape of the opening is due to the fact that this form is the strongest natural configuration. Other shapes usually fall apart quickly from erosion.

The Oak Creek Fault is easy to see at this location. Look north (up canyon) and notice the difference in the height of the corresponding rock layers from the east to the west side of the creek. The west wall's rock units are obviously higher relative to the east wall.

For more information about the park, contact: Park Manager, Slide Rock State Park, P.O. Box 10358, Sedona, AZ 86336; (602) 282-3034.

As you continue south, look up to the right (west) and you may catch a glimpse of a natural arch in the Schnebly Hill Formation. A better and safer view is from the State Park parking lot. Blackberries and poison ivy grow profusely along the road in here.

Opposite the north end of the **Manzanita Campground** is the **Sterling Pass Trail** (MP 380.5). An early resident by the name of Sterling allegedly kept counterfeiting equipment in a cabin near the pass. The trail is said to follow an old Indian route and eventually leads to Sterling Canyon in the Dry Creek Basin to the west.

Another mile down the highway brings one to the **Encinoso Picnic Area** and the **North Wilson Trailhead** (MP 379.4). This trail climbs through a lovely forested canyon and intersects the Wilson Mountain (South Wilson) Trail on First Bench where you may see "volcanic bombs," tear-drop shaped pieces of lava formed when molten magma was ejected through the air. The trail continues on to the top of Wilson Mountain.

Continue south for less than a mile and you come to the **Creekside Mobile Village**. Immediately south of its driveway, you may work your way down to the creek and wade across to the **Thompson Ladder Trail** (MP 378.6), which climbs the north side of Munds Canyon. The "ladder" refers to the way the upper part of the trail rises in a series of steps. The trail originally began at the Thompson homestead in the bottom of the canyon. Today the beginning of this trail is not very well defined since it has been re-routed to avoid private land. James Munds homesteaded near the head of this canyon in 1883.

The Canyon broadens a great deal below the mouth of Munds Canyon. In a moment you enter a shady spot known as **Indian Gardens** (MP 378.2). This is Natural History Stop 4.

Natural History Stop 4
INDIAN GARDENS

Elevation: 4570 feet   Milepost 378.2

Walk a little south of the Indian Gardens Trading Post and General Store, turn around, and look to the northeast. The eastern wall of the canyon towers above the Arizona black walnuts, Arizona sycamores, box elders, and elderberries in the foreground. Most of the upper wall is composed of successive layers of basalt or lava. Can you make out seven distinct layers? Each individual ledge of lava probably represents a separate flow, the oldest being about eight million years. The uppermost or youngest volcanic layers have not yet been dated but are believed to be about five million years old.

Often in the spring as the deep snows along the rim melt, several waterfalls develop along this particular wall, but most of the year these sun-baked canyon walls are bone dry. The chaparral vegetation consists of two species of silk-tassel bush, Apache plume, cliffrose, mountain mahogany, two species of manzanita, some catclaw acacia, buckbrush, and abundant thickets of shrub live oak.

Across from the Indian Gardens Trading Post under a huge Arizona sycamore is an historical marker about John Jim Thompson, one of Oak Creek's earliest settlers. Prior to Thompson's arrival,

Yavapai/Apache Indians farmed this part of the canyon. About eighteen Indian families lived here sporadically until 1903.

Continue down the highway to lower Oak Creek Canyon.

Cassin's Kingbird

LOWER OAK CREEK CANYON MAP

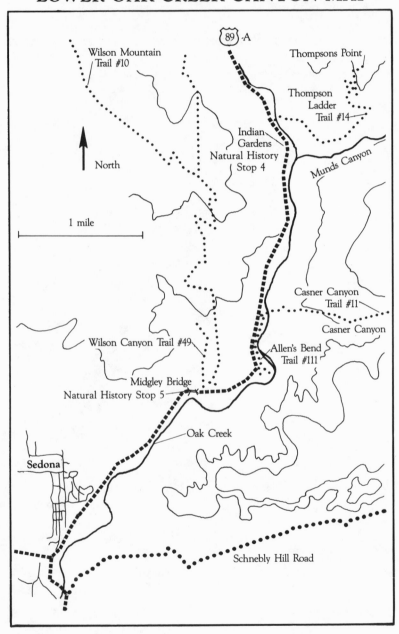

LOWER CANYON

Indian Gardens to Sedona

Another early resident of Oak Creek was John James (Jim) Thompson who settled at Indian Gardens in 1876. Thompson had immigrated alone from Ireland in 1852 at the tender age of eleven. He traveled across the nation to Texas, down into Mexico, up to Utah and finally to Arizona. At that time the area was known as Bacon Rind Park, but Thompson's place eventually became known as Indian Gardens. Some say that Thompson had as neighbors a few Yavapai/Apache Indian families who grew crops, hence the name, Indian Gardens. Others say that the Yavapai/Apaches who had been raising crops here were rounded up by U.S. Army troops from Fort Verde. He filed for a homestead, giving the best directions that he could, but when the land was surveyed by the General Land Office about 1900, it was discovered that his description was for a piece of land atop Wilson Mountain. Thompson refiled for the land he called home, using an accurate legal description the second time.

At his prompting, ranching friends from Nevada, the James family, moved to the area with a small herd of cattle in May, 1878. Two years later, their daughter, Margaret, married Thompson. Although it is only a few miles up the canyon, Indian Gardens was so difficult to reach in those days that Thompson didn't move his family there until 1887. If he could only see it now!

(Note: There is always danger of a snag or two when spinning a yarn—a common problem with oral histories. The details for the above historical events vary a bit from source to source. The Oak Creek Canyon area is ripe for a scholarly historical account.)

From Indian Gardens (MP 378.2) to Sedona, Oak Creek Canyon becomes even more spectacular. About a mile south of Indian Gardens, Casner Canyon enters from the east. The red rocks of the Schnebly Hill, Hermit, and Supai formations begin to dominate the landscape with buttes, spires, and other fanciful forms. In order to give them this stunning color only one-half of one percent of the composition of the rocks has to be

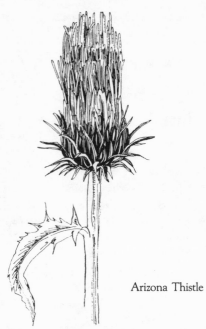

Arizona Thistle

iron oxide. In the old days, cowboys called this vermilion country "Hell's Hollow."

Oak Creek flows through an inner gorge cut into the Supai Formation while the highway traverses the lower edge of the Hermit Shale. An Arizona cypress woodland mantles the shale slope and thins out on the higher and steeper Schnebly Hill Formation.

In the late 1870s, Moses and Riley Casner built a cattle trail up this canyon to the rim. You can still follow it today although the head of the trail near the mouth of Casner has been washed out a bit (MP 376.9). In 1973, 565 acres of **Casner Canyon** were designated a Research Natural Area by the Forest Service in order to preserve a representative stand of Arizona cypress.

At the **Grasshopper Point** Day-Use Area (MP 376.7), the short but pleasant **Allen's Bend Trail** begins. This route meanders through an old orchard located between the creek and red sandstone cliffs. There is a lot of shade, so it is a pleasant hike in the summer.

Returning to the highway, drive around the bend to the east end of the **Midgley Bridge** (MP 376.1). Two trails start here: the **(South) Wilson Mountain Trail** and **Wilson Canyon Trail**. This is Natural History Stop 5.

Natural History Stop 5
MIDGLEY BRIDGE

Elevation: 4520 feet   Milepost 376.1

Midgley Bridge was named after Flagstaff resident William Midgley who spearheaded the movement to build a bridge across Wilson Canyon. Before the bridge was dedicated in 1939, travel into and out of Oak Creek Canyon was sometimes impossible after a rain storm or during snow melt. The Arizona Department of Transportation recently nominated the bridge to the National Register of Historic Places.

To the north is Wilson Mountain which dramatically displays the Coconino Sandstone. A lava cap of columnar jointed basalt is also evident. Note how First Bench to the right of Wilson is a down-faulted piece of the mountain. The Oak Creek Fault cuts right through the pass on the skyline. This is one of several places in Oak Creek Canyon where the creek did not follow the fault in its excavation of the canyon. Also, at this location the Oak Creek Fault makes a right angle jog to the east whereas the creek (and canyon) continues a southerly flow. That accounts for the rather sudden appearance of red rocks on both sides of the highway. Remember that up canyon the Schnebly Hill Formation is primarily on the west side, all the red rock layers having been down-faulted on the east side.

In the foreground, the higher red rock, such as Steamboat Rock, is composed of the Schnebly Hill Formation; the reddish, tree-covered slopes are Hermit Shale; and the inner gorge beneath the bridge is the Supai Formation. In previous geologic accounts (including my earlier book on Oak Creek), the red rocks are usually denoted as being all Supai; but recent work done by Northern Arizona University geologist Ron Blakey and others has shown that only the lower red rocks are Supai, a formation well- studied in the Grand Canyon.

The Hermit Shale is also recognized in the Grand Canyon; however, the Schnebly Hill Formation is unique to the area southeast of the Grand Canyon. Also, the formation that a few geologists formerly called Redwall Limestone within Oak Creek Canyon is now thought to be localized limestone deposits along faults or fractures in the Supai. This is probably of little consequence to the average tourist passing through northern Arizona; but to the locals, the rock walls and buttes have become old friends. And, as with our other friends, we are always curious about their background.

Beautiful stands of Arizona cypress cover the slopes here. Other plants include sugar sumac, juniper, mountain mahogany, deerbrush ceanothus, manzanita, catclaw acacia, shrub live oak, buckbrush, barberry, prickly pear, false paloverde or canotia, agave, and yucca. Scrub jays, pinyon jays and ravens are common.

There are two trails that start here. The (South) Wilson Mountain Trail, which has been designated a National Recreation Trail, climbs more than 2000 feet to the top of Wilson Mountain and features exceptional vistas. National Recreation Trail status ensures the protection and maintenance of this scenic trail. The second route, Wilson Canyon Trail, follows the drainage in front of you toward the base of Wilson Mountain. This is an easy way to get an intimate look at the cypress woodland.

Wilson Mountain and the canyon are named after Richard Wilson. In June 1885 he was hunting a grizzly bear which he apparently wounded. The bear charged and the hunter became the hunted. Wilson's badly-mauled body was found several days later.

Another few miles brings you to the hamlet of **Sedona** and the end of Oak Creek Canyon. This is not, however, the last of the Red Rock Country.

Continue through town to the stoplight and turn left onto State Highway 179. Pass the shopping center of Tlaquepaque (on your right), and cross the creek. Immediately after crossing the creek, **Schnebly Hill Road** (FR 153) is on the left. This very scenic Forest Service road offers fine views and an eleven-mile alternative (in dry weather and for high-clearance vehicles) to reach Interstate 17.

As you start up the dirt road, you are traveling along **Bear Wallow Canyon**. The blue-green foliage of Arizona cypress contrasts sharply with the red sandstone cliffs. As the road climbs higher, the woodland gives way to chaparral.

Bear Wallow Canyon follows a major fault. Notice that the rock units to your right (south) are several hundred feet lower than the corresponding units on the left. For example, the buff-colored Coconino Sandstone on your left is found only as a remnant at the very top of the red buttes. To the right, the soaring, tan cliff-face is the Coconino Sandstone and the underlying red Schnebly Hill Formation is mostly hidden.

At the head of Bear Wallow Canyon, just below a point where you can see an old alignment of the road switchbacking up to the rim, there is a good view of the Fort Apache Limestone at Merry- go-round Rock. The prominent gray ledge is the resistant limestone within the Schnebly Hill Formation and represents an incursion of an ancient sea.

If it has been a wet spring and summer, common roadside wildflowers will include pink, red, and magenta penstemons, sacred datura or jimson weed, yellow-flowered prickly pear, New Mexico locust, ceanothus, orange Indian paintbrush, and coyote melon.

Sacred Datura

After reaching the rim, there are several dirt roads leading off into the forest; most are in terrible condition and not suitable for passenger cars. Not quite two miles into the ponderosa pines, Forest Road 801 turns off to the right (south) and goes about four miles to the **Munds Mountain Trailhead** (Forest Trail –77; see trail chart in Red Rock South chapter). This trail is a main entrance into the newly-established, 18,150-acre Munds Mountain Wilderness Area.

The main Schnebly Hill Road continues past a lovely pond where great blue herons, snowy egrets, and other shore birds may be seen. The road then crosses a piece of private property, the **Foxboro Ranch**. The ranch was built about 1926 and was originally used as a tourist resort. Foxboro

Ranch was very popular, especially when Mayhew's Lodge at the mouth of West Fork was full. Another two miles and you arrive at Interstate 17.

If you don't take the Schnebly Hill Road after Tlaquepaque, you may continue down Highway 179 to visit the Red Rock South area. Or, back at the stoplight, continue on Highway 89A toward West Sedona and the options to be found there which are described in the "Secret Mountains and Canyons" chapter following.

Green-backed Heron

TRAIL CHART FOR OAK CREEK CANYON

Please stay on trails where they exist. Also respect private land; do not trespass. For further trail information, contact the Sedona Ranger District, P.O. Box 300, 225 Brewer Road, Sedona, AZ 86336; (602) 282-4119 and/or consult: *Oak Creek Canyon and the Red Rock Country of Arizona* by Aitchison.

TRAIL CHART FOR OAK CREEK CANYON

Name (USFS Trail #)	Trailhead Location	Length (one-way miles)	Climb (feet)	Features
Cookstove (143)	MP 387.0	0.7 (to rim)	800	Rim can be followed to Harding Springs Trail
Harding Springs (51)	MP 385.9	0.7 (to rim)	700	Built in early 1880s by J.R. Robinson, later improved by Dave Hart (1883) and Col. O.P. Harding (1893). Springs are located about 0.4 mile north of trailhead.
Thomas Point (142)	MP 384.5	1.0 (to rim)	800	Built in early 1880s by C.S. (Bear) Howard
West Fork (108)	MP 384.5	3.0 (13.0 to FR 231)	300	Scenic, nar- row canyon, wading required
A.B. Young (100) (East Pocket)	MP 383.1	2.4 (to lookout)	2000	Originally a cattle trail, later improved by Civilian Conserva- tion Corps during the 1930s.
Sterling Pass (46)	MP 380.5	2.4	1120	Route over to Sterling Canyon in the Dry Creek Basin.
North Wilson (123)	MP 379.4	2.0	1700	Probably established around 1890 when J.J. Thompson, a homesteader near Indian Gardens, grazed horses on top of the mountain.
Thompson Ladder (14)	MP 378.6	1.5 (to rim)	1400	Built by Richard Wilson in 1880s when he became stranded on east side of a flooding Oak Creek.
Casner Canyon (11)	MP 376.9	2.0	1400	Cattle trail built by Moses and Riley Casner dur- ing 1877-78.
Allen's Bend (111)	Grasshopper Point Recreation Site	0.5	level	Old orchard
Wilson Mountain (South Wilson) (10)	MP 376.1	5.6	2300	Great views of Verde Valley, Oak Creek, San Francisco Peaks.
Wilson Canyon (49)	MP 376.1	Up to 1.0	400	Where bear hunter Richard Wilson was killed by a grizzly in June 1885.

SECRET MTNS. AND CANYONS MAP

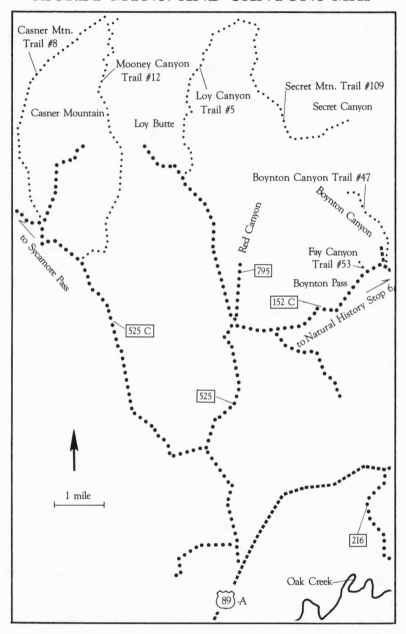

Casner Mtn.
Trail #8

Mooney Canyon
Trail #12

Loy Canyon
Trail #5

Secret Mtn. Trail #109

Secret Canyon

Casner Mountain

Loy Butte

Boynton Canyon Trail #47

Boynton Canyon

Red Canyon

Fay Canyon
Trail #53

to Sycamore Pass

795

Boynton Pass

152 C

to Natural History Stop 6

525 C

525

1 mile

216

Oak Creek

89 -A

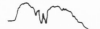

CHAPTER 2

SECRET MOUNTAINS
AND CANYONS

*The colors of the rocks are variegated, so that the gorgeous cliffs appear
to be banded, rising from 800 to 1000 feet sheer on all sides. These rocks
had weathered into fantastic shapes suggestive of cathedrals, Greek
temples, and sharp steeples of churches extending like giant needles into
the sky . . . This place, I have no doubt, will sooner or later become
popular with the sightseer, and I regard the discovery of these cliffs one
of the most interesting of my summer's field work.*

Jesse Walter Fewkes,
Archeological Expedition to Arizona in 1895, 1896

Northwest of Sedona is the escarpment of the Mogollon Rim, the
southern edge of the Colorado Plateau. Numerous drainages have cut back
into the Rim to form a maze of deep, narrow canyons. Many of these
secret places are easily accessible by vehicle and foot.

On the north edge of **West Sedona** is the collapsed cave or sinkhole
called the Devil's Kitchen. To get there, drive west on U.S. Highway 89A
about 1.3 miles from the stoplight at the intersection of Highways 89A
and 179. Turn north onto Soldier Pass Road at the east end of Grasshopper Flat. In a mile and a half, turn right onto Rim Shadow Drive
and follow the "forest access" signs to the Soldier Pass Trailhead. The
Soldier Pass Trail is an old jeep route that is better suited to feet than
to tires. Follow the trail a few hundred feet to a major fork. Take the right

branch down across the wash and up the other side to find the **Devil's Kitchen.**

Returning to Highway 89A, continue west across Grasshopper Flat and through West Sedona. To your left (south) is **Table Top Mountain** (also called Airport Mesa) which may be an ancient delta deposited by Oak Creek several million years ago when the Verde Valley was filled by a lake. As you drive up the airport road onto the mesa, notice that most of the rocks are dark gray basalt boulders that have been rounded by being tumbled in moving water. These boulders probably originated on the Mogollon Rim to the north, but further study is needed to confirm this hypothesis. Small rounded pebbles of the softer sedimentary rocks of Oak Creek Canyon are also mixed in the deposit. At the west end of Grasshopper Flat, turn right (north) onto the **Dry Creek Road** (MP 371.0). Set your trip meter to zero or note your odometer reading.

At 2.0 miles, a dirt road (Dry Creek Road, FR 152) branches to the right. This rough road is passable to high-clearance cars provided it hasn't rained recently and you drive slowly. Four established Forest Service trails— Devil's Bridge, Brins Mesa, Secret Canyon, and Vultee Arch—and numerous cross-country routes are waiting for the hiker who wants to explore the Red Rock-Secret Mountain Wilderness Area.

Returning to the paved road, which from this point on is called the **Boynton Pass Road** (FR 152C), continue a few hundred feet until you have a good view to the northwest. This is Natural History Stop 6.

Ringtail cat

Natural History Stop 6
BOYNTON PASS ROAD

Elevation: 4600 feet   Mileage from Sedona: about two miles

Dry Creek and its tributaries form a broad, open basin—nothing like the narrow Oak Creek Canyon. Yet both creeks have cut through the same rock layers. The difference is due primarily to the fact that the rim of Oak Creek is protected by a thick layer of basalt and the Dry Creek rim is not. Without the lava cap, erosion has been able to quickly attack the relatively soft sedimentary rocks and cut back farther into the rim.

At this stop, you can see the isolated buttes and mesas between Secret, Long, and Boynton Canyons. Maroon Mountain in particular stands tall and remote, home to the golden eagle and other cliff nesters.

If you are having difficulty distinguishing where the exact contact is between the Hermit Shale and Schnebly Hill Formation or between the Schnebly Hill and Coconino Sandstone, don't worry. There is no sharp contact. If you are familiar with the Grand Canyon's geology, you know that there is a very distinct break between the Coconino and the underlying Hermit; there is no Schnebly Hill. That break, or unconformity as geologists call such things, denotes a period of erosion. Here in the Red Rock Country there was continual deposition from Hermit time through Coconino time; there was just a gradual change in environments from a floodplain to a desert with no period of erosion. The result is a gradational change from Hermit to Schnebly Hill to Coconino. As geologist Wayne Ranney says, "Geologists sometimes try to draw lines between formations where there are no lines." So just relax and enjoy the scenery.

Several million years ago, the Verde Lake reached as far as where the road crosses Dry Creek just down the hill from here. The rolling hills along the road are composed of Hermit Shale and are covered by dense woodlands of Arizona cypress, pinyon pine and juniper. Shrub live oak, barberry, buckbrush, manzanita, silk-tassel bush,

Black-headed Grosbeak

and other scrubby bushes form an almost impenetrable understory. If you explore the canyons in the spring, expect to find penstemon, blue dicks, evening primrose, flax, spring beauty, lupine, wallflower, golden pea, heron bill, lousewort, and Indian paintbrush. In the higher reaches of these canyons, ponderosa pine, Douglas fir, alligator-bark juniper, Oregon grape, birchleaf buckthorn, Gambel oak, and mountain mahogany intermingle.

Although birds are not as numerous here as they are along Oak Creek, the patient birder will hear or see scrub jays, pinyon jays, ravens, turkey vultures, rufous-sided towhees, bridled titmice, black-throated gray warblers, white-throated swifts, acorn woodpeckers, Bewick's wrens, rock wrens, Bell's vireos, and black-throated sparrows.

Rock squirrels are fairly common, too. They may be confused with Arizona gray squirrels, but the rock squirrel's fur is grayish, mottled overall with cinnamon, while the Arizona gray has a light brown or ochraceous middle back. Also, rock squirrels tend to carry their tails straight out behind, whereas the Arizona gray will curl its tail up.

Continue across Dry Creek to the T-intersection. The right branch provides access to **Long Canyon Trail**; the left branch continues to yet another intersection. From the T-intersection, the paved road on the right leads to John Gardiner's Enchantment (also called Boynton Canyon Ranch). Just before reaching the resort guardhouse, you will see a pullout on the right for the **Boynton Canyon Trailhead**. There are many prehistoric cliff dwellings in Boynton (look but don't touch), a canyon that holds special significance to the Yavapai/Apache Indians.

> From the underworld, all humans and animals ascended on the first maize plant. The hole through which they came then filled with water and is today called Montezuma's Well. After the second world was destroyed by fire, a flood destroyed the third world. One person, Kamalapukwia, survived inside a hollow agave stalk that settled in Boynton Canyon. She lived in a cave and soon became impregnated by Sun and Cloud and bore a daughter. This daughter also became impregnated by Sun and Cloud and had a son, Lofty Wanderer. He called all the creatures of the world together in a cave in Hartwell Canyon and taught each their right ways and then sent the different races of man to the far corners of the world. The Wipukpaya (Yavapai/Apache) alone stayed at the Center of the World where everything had begun.
>
> Wipukpaya (Yavapai/Apache) Legend

The Wipukpaya also speak of the "little people" who inhabit the Red Rocks. They are about three feet tall, have round heads, eyes and a mouth, but no nose. They wear skirts of fresh juniper twigs and can sometimes appear as a whirlwind or be heard hollering in the canyons.

Traditions of these "people at the foot of the mountains" recall their origins in the Red Rock Country. The Wipukpaya lived in caves or pole-domed huts thatched with grass. The base may have been covered with dirt and the top of the dome made waterproof with animal hides. Shades or ramadas were often used during the hot summer.

As time passed, they began to plant a little maize, beans, squash, and tobacco in moist areas such as Indian Gardens and West Fork, but primarily they continued to hunt game and gather wild plant foods. Their greatest food supply was harvested in the fall when acorns, pinyon nuts, black walnuts, sunflower seeds, goldeneye seeds, wild grasses, manzanita berries, juniper berries, hackberries, squawberries, wild grapes, cactus fruits, mesquite beans, and the fruit of the banana yucca were harvested. The agave plant was an important year-round food source. It was dug up, the leaves cut off, and the "heart" roasted in a pit for several days. It was eaten or dried and stored for future use. Wipukpaya families may have spent three to four months in one area gathering and preparing agaves.

In May, 1583, Antonio de Espejo, the first non-Indian in the area, entered the Verde Valley and found people wearing "crowns of painted sticks on their heads and jicaras [small bowls] of mescal and pinyon nuts and bread made from it." In 1598, the Spaniard Marcos Farfan de los Godos encountered people wearing small wooden crosses on their heads and labeled them Cruzados. By the 1900s, confusion by Anglo settlers and some government officials had led to these people being called everything from Yavapai/Apache to Apache/Mohave.

Today, the Wipukpaya are considered one of the four subgroups of the Yavapai. Their descendants live on the Camp Verde, Middle Verde, and Clarkdale Reservations. (The traditional name for the Northeastern Yavapai is variously spelled Wipukpaya, Wipukupa or Wipukyipai. See Khera and Mariella, 1983 for more background on the confusing origins of names for these people.)

Back at the T-intersection, the left road is dirt and heads southwest past the mouth of **Fay Canyon** where a small stand of western soapberry trees grows. Follow Fay Canyon Trail about a half-mile to where a footpath on the right leads to a natural arch with a small prehistoric Sinagua ruin under it.

Perhaps as long ago as eight thousand years, nomadic hunters passed through the Red Rock Country gathering wild plant foods and hunting bighorn sheep, deer, and elk. We know almost nothing about these enigmatic people, and all that remains of them today are a few tools and spearpoints made of a stone that is not native to the area.

The first permanent residents who archaeologists know something about were the Sinagua, a termed coined by Dr. Harold S. Colton, founder of Flagstaff's Museum of Northern Arizona. He used an early Spanish name for the San Francisco Peaks meaning "without water" to name these people. The name also describes their pursuit of an agrarian lifestyle that relied on rainfall rather than irrigation to grow crops, a type of agriculture known as dry farming.

By the late seventh century A.D., the Sinagua were occupying the Red Rock Country, the Verde Valley, and the Flagstaff region. The Sinagua hunted rabbit, deer, and bighorn sheep, and gathered wild plants such as agave, pinyon nuts, yucca fruit, walnuts, mesquite beans, and prickly pear; but their attention was increasingly turning to growing corn, beans, and squash, both in the lowlands and on mesa tops. Two or three centuries later, the technology of irrigation agriculture appeared in the Verde

Palmer's Penstemon

Valley. Additional characteristics appearing in the valley at that time suggest influences, and perhaps people, from the Hohokam culture in the Salt River Valley around Phoenix.

Throughout most of their history, the Sinagua lived in pithouses, partly-subterranean dwellings with brush and pole sides. An entrance through the roof also served as a smoke hole. By A.D. 1000 the burgeoning population was gathering into cooperative groups to build pueblos or villages. At some sites, large pithouses, platform mounds, and ball courts indicate the locations of important centers for the Verde Valley.

The years between A.D. 1050 and 1130 were unusually wet and warm, and harvests must have been relatively bountiful. The warmer mesa tops provided a slightly longer growing season than the valley floor and were intensely farmed. The population continued to expand and the construction of hilltop communities such as Tuzigoot began. The valley residents had salt from the Verde Lake deposits, copper from near the present site of Jerome, and the brittle claystone argillite which they used in jewelry. They also cultivated cotton to trade for parrot feathers, sea shells, and pottery.

These several hundred years of prosperity ended with abandonment of the area in the 1400s. Why or where these people went is still uncertain. It is known that during the 1400s, the Yavapai/Apache people entered the area to hunt and gather wild plant foods. Did these new residents displace the old? Or did Sinagua society evolve and merge into the Yavapai/Apache people?

Virtually all cliff sites in the Red Rock Country have been molested or vandalized. Every time another artifact is removed, a hole dug, or a wall pushed down, another piece in the puzzle of the past is destroyed. State and federal laws protect these antiquities and provide penalties for those who would steal and destroy our heritage. If you happen upon ruins or relics of these ancient people, please do not disturb or collect anything. Your help in protecting these fragile fragments of history will aid in the unraveling of the mysteries of the past.

Let's continue now with our travels. The road climbs over **Boynton Pass**, providing a view of Mingus Mountain, part of Arizona's Black Hills. Up to this point you have been traveling through a fairly dense woodland of Arizona cypress, pinyon pine, and juniper. Notice that the cypress and pinyons disappear ahead. Juniper and mesquite are the dominant trees with narrowleaf yucca, squawbush, and catclaw acacia making up the understory. There are also more open fields or parks.

Plateau whiptail lizard

Two unmarked trails take off from near the pass—one heads up **Bear Mountain**; the other climbs **Doe Mountain**. Contact the Sedona Ranger Station for the latest information regarding these two routes.

This is a good area to look for reptiles during the summer and, after a rain, amphibians. Herptiles, as they are collectively called, abound in the Red Rock Country; but this is no reason to stay in your car. They are not disgusting, slimy creatures, but rather, remarkable animals that have evolved to cope with their harsh desert environment.

Among the Red Rocks, you can find such oddities as the plateau whiptail lizard, which comes only in the female gender. These lizards reproduce parthenogenetically; that is, their eggs are stimulated to develop without male input. You may also see a short-horned lizard (incorrectly called a horned toad), which can squirt blood out of its eyes if molested. And don't miss the harmless gopher snake which can do a better than fair imitation of a rattlesnake by flattening its head and shaking its tail. Three of the most common lizards—eastern fence, side-blotched, and tree—are difficult to distinguish from one other: all are small and brown colored. The bright blue-green collared lizard, on the other hand, is easy to recognize.

Snakes are generally not encountered and would prefer it that way. Since they don't have legs, they are very vulnerable to the hot ground temperatures that can occur on even a mild day. Rattlesnakes generally avoid being out in the direct sunlight and are therefore more active at night. Their flicking tongues help them smell their surroundings by capturing odors and bringing them to two tiny openings in the roof of the mouth. Rattlesnakes also have temperature-sensitive organs located in pits between their eyes and nostrils which help them locate their warm-blooded prey.

The spadefoot toad spends most of its life underground in a torpid state. When the summer rains come, the toads emerge to sing and copulate. Eggs are laid in the temporary rainpools and begin to hatch into tadpoles. The sun heats the water which speeds the metamorphosis along. Many of the young tadpoles die and their decaying bodies release hormones that also enhance the process of changing. If the pool does not dry up too rapidly, the remaining tadpoles become toads and hop off to dig into the dirt and wait for another rainy day.

Not far beyond Boynton Pass, **Marshall Tank** appears on the left. Several large Fremont cottonwoods provide shade for the cattle that graze nearby and come here to drink.

Spadefoot toad

A few more miles and you intersect **Forest Road 525**. If you turn right, FR 525 leads to several fascinating areas. In just a few tenths of a mile after the junction, you will intersect **FR 795** which leads to **Red Canyon** and Palatki or Red House, a well-preserved Sinagua ruin. The Forest Service requests that you contact the Sedona Ranger Station for information regarding access to this special site.

About 2.4 miles down FR 525 is the unmarked turnoff to **Hartwell Canyon**, a new addition to the list of preserves of the Arizona Nature Conservancy (a chapter of the international Nature Conservancy). To visit Hartwell, contact: Arizona Nature Conservancy, P.O. Box 40326, Tucson, AZ 85717; (602) 622-3861 or (602) 867-7225.

Another 1.3 miles brings you to the **Loy Canyon Trail**, which leads to the top of Secret Mountain.

To visit Honanki or **Bear House**, a thirteenth-century Sinagua cliff dwelling, drive about .7 of a mile beyond the Loy Canyon trailhead through the Hancock Ranch and pull off to the right on a little dirt track to reach a parking area. Please remember that this is private property and no camping or campfires are permitted. Follow the short path to the ruin located against the base of Loy Butte.

Returning to the junction of FR 525 and Boynton Pass Road (FR 152C), turn south (left) on FR 525 to return to Highway 89A. As you approach the highway, the vegetation becomes less dense. One-seed juniper, false paloverde, and mesquite are well-spaced, indicating that there is little ground moisture.

About 2.7 miles before reaching the highway, FR 525C leads off northwesterly to the **Sycamore Canyon Wilderness** and trailheads at Mooney Canyon, Casner Mountain, and Sycamore Pass.

Another scenic route west of Sedona is the **Red Rock Upper Loop Road** (FR 216). Starting at the intersection of Highways 179 and 89A, drive a little more than four miles west on 89A and turn left onto the Red Rock Upper Loop Road (MP 370.1). This paved road winds down through catclaw, banana yucca, false paloverde, juniper, and some pinyon for 1.9 miles to an intersection. The left fork, FR 216A, takes you to the old **Red Rock** (or Baldwin's) **Crossing**, probably the most photographed location in the entire Sedona area. This is Natural History Stop 7. You can no longer cross the creek with your vehicle, but the national forest day-use area is an excellent spot for wading, sunning, and picnicking. The stream-side ("riparian") vegetation offers outstanding birding.

Natural History Stop 7
RED ROCK CROSSING

Elevation: 3950 feet   Mileage from Sedona: about 6.5 miles

The imposing butte in the background was originally named Courthouse Rock or Butte, but due to an error on the 1886 General Land Office Survey Map, it is now known as Cathedral Rock. The butte is composed of Schnebly Hill Formation rock even though you are now several hundred feet lower in elevation than Steamboat Rock or The Thumb near Midgley Bridge. Several major faults between here and Sedona account for the lowering of the rock layers.

But why is this relatively isolated butte here at all? There is a remnant of a volcanic dike running up the west slope to the notch and some geologists think that several million years ago lava may have reached the surface and flowed out, forming a protective basalt cap. Erosion stripped away the relatively softer surrounding sedimentary rock leaving a mesa. The lava cap has now been eroded away and the mesa reduced to a butte. Come back a million or so years from now and Cathedral Rock will be gone.

Along lower Oak Creek, the riparian vegetation is considerably different from the upper end. Warmer temperatures (Sedona has never recorded a below zero temperature) allow narrowleaf cottonwood to be replaced by Fremont cottonwood, and the conifers are replaced with deciduous, broad-leafed trees like Arizona sycamore plus desert species such as mesquite and catclaw acacia. Some species manage to live in both the upper and lower riparian habitats. These include Arizona walnut, Arizona alder, velvet ash, box elder, arroyo willow, red willow, wild grape, poison ivy, river sedge, and horsetail. A wide variety of wildflowers make their debut each spring and summer.

Also along the stream and washes is what is called Lowell ash, a pinnately compound-leafed variety of the common desert or single-leaf ash. For a time this ash was thought to be a separate species found only in central Arizona (i.e. an endemic to this area). Botanists now believe that it is within the genetic variability of desert ash. Flagstaff astronomer Percival Lowell, who studied the "canals" of Mars, was also a botanist and discovered this ash in Oak Creek in the late 1800s.

Northern Arizona University biologist Dean Blinn is impressed with the great diversity of algae and aquatic insects that are found in Oak Creek. He believes the primary factor in determining the richness of species is the tremendous gradient or fall that the creek has from its source to its confluence with the Verde River. The creek drops vertically more than a half-mile in about sixty miles—an average gradient of fifty feet per mile. By comparison, the Colorado River falls an average of only eight feet per mile through the Grand Canyon. Entomologist Milton Sanderson has suggested classifying Oak Creek as "Endangered Waters" in order to call attention to the fact that this is a special and unique aquatic habitat deserving our best care.

Desert riparian habitats are extremely important to birds. The permanent water allows many species of trees to grow. Without these trees, the majority of birds found in the desert would have no place to nest. There are relatively few ground-nesting or cliff-nesting species.

Not only is there a great variety of birds within riparian habitats, the density of breeding pairs for a given space can be phenomenal. A study done in the upper riparian zone of Oak Creek showed a respectable 365 pairs per 100 acres. On a study area in a fairly pure stand of cottonwoods along the Verde River, an incredible 847 pairs per 100 acres were counted!

Brown-crested Flycatcher

(Compare this figure with approximately 200 pairs of birds per 100 acres in an average eastern deciduous forest, and the importance of desert riparian habitats becomes clear.) Similar high densities of breeding birds may occur along lower Oak Creek.

The list on p. 97 of the birds you can expect along lower Oak Creek reveals the exceptional diversity of species to be found in this area.

For more detailed bird information and birding trips of the local area, contact the Northern Arizona Audubon Society, P.O. Box 1496, Sedona, AZ 86336.

As Oak Creek makes its dash toward the Verde River, the water has plenty of time to warm under the Arizona sun. Consequently, the trout and other cold water fish of the upper canyon are replaced by warm water species farther downstream.

Four species of catfish—channel, yellow, black, and flathead, all exotics— inhabit lower Oak Creek. Other non-native fish include fathead minnows, red shiners, mosquito fish, largemouth bass, rock bass, and the ubiquitous carp. Ironically, carp were first introduced into Arizona waters prior to 1885 with the hope that they would become a valuable food fish. Perhaps the most important game fish of lower Oak Creek is the smallmouth bass.

The native Colorado River chub, Gila sucker, spike dace (now listed as a threatened species and probably only occurring in the upper Verde from Clarkdale upstream), and Colorado River squawfish used to be common. Today the squawfish has been essentially eliminated from Arizona waters and is considered endangered in other parts of the Colorado River Basin. The chub is one of the few native fish that seems to be able to maintain its population in spite of introduced game fish.

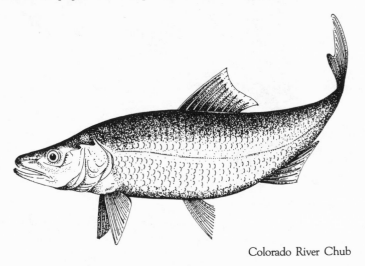

Colorado River Chub

Back at the junction on the Red Rock Upper Loop Road, the right fork is the main Red Rock Upper Loop, FR 216. Cross the cattle guard and the road becomes dirt. This loop circles the basalt-capped Schuerman Mountain, passing a number of private homes and ranches. The mountain is named after John George Heinrich (Henry) Schuerman, a German who in 1885 settled an old debt of $500 by accepting a 160-acre farm on Oak Creek.

In spite of civilization pressing directly up against the boundaries of the Coconino National Forest, reclusive black bear and mountain lion still haunt the Red Rock Country. During the day, you are most likely to see tree squirrels such as Abert's, Arizona gray and red; cliff and gray-collared chipmunks; rock squirrels, golden-mantled ground squirrels, and Harris' antelope squirrels. Most of the mammals are nocturnal or crepuscular (i.e. active at twilight).

Nocturnal mammals can avoid the extreme temperatures of the day and avoid being seen by many potential predators. The diurnal squirrels have the advantage of being able to climb trees to escape both predators and the hot ground. Additionally, the desert-dwelling squirrels have the ability to withstand an elevated body temperature that would cause brain damage in other mammals.

Two species of deer roam the Red Rock Country. Coues white- tailed deer, a distinctly smaller subspecies than their eastern cousins, tend to range in the lower canyon areas (a small herd lives near Slide Rock), whereas mule deer are more often found in the higher forest.

The native Merriam's elk was hunted to extinction prior to 1920. The elk you see today along the rim country were imported from Yellowstone National Park.

One mammal whose spoor is often seen is the much maligned coyote. Though relentlessly hunted, trapped, and poisoned, the adaptable "desert dog" has actually expanded its range across North America. The coyote serves a valuable role in the ecosystem by controlling rabbit, squirrel and other rodent populations.

About a half-mile farther down FR 216 on the right is the old pioneer cemetery where John Jim Thompson has been laid to rest among other early Oak Creek settlers.

Coues white-tailed deer

Another two-and-a-half miles away is the entrance to the **Red Rock State Park** which at the time of this writing is still in the development stage and not open to the public. In December 1986, this 286-acre parcel of land—the Old Smoke Trail Ranch on lower Oak Creek—was added to the state park system. According to Duane Miller, a member of the Arizona State Parks Board, the original idea of turning this land into a park came from then Governor Bruce Babbitt. Bald eagles winter here, and in the spring Mexican black hawks have nested. Mammals found here include gray fox, javelina, raccoons, beaver, muskrat, and pocket gopher. The park will be oriented toward nature study and recreational activities such as hiking, horseback riding, and bicycling. For the latest information contact: Park Manager, Red Rock State Park, P.O. Box 3864, West Sedona, AZ 86340; (602) 282-6907.

Three miles more brings you back out onto Highway 89A. Look across the highway to the west (left) and you will see a dark cone-shaped hill; it is an ancient volcanic dike or intrusion of magma that squeezed up along the Cathedral Fault, one of the major faults between this point and Sedona.

Common Black Hawk

TRAIL CHART FOR
SECRET MOUNTAINS AND CANYONS

Name (USFS Trail #)	Trailhead Location	Length (one-way miles)	Climb (feet)	Features
Devil's Kitchen	See Soldier Pass	0.25	75	Sinkhole 65 feet deep, 112 feet across; formed in 1880s when cave ceiling collapsed.
Soldier Pass (66)	Follow forest access signs at end of Soldier Pass Road	2.0 to pass	450	
Devil's Bridge (120)	FR 152	0.9	400	
Brins Mesa (119)	FR 152			
Secret Canyon (121)	FR 152	5.0	600	
Vultee Arch (22)	End of FR 152	1.7	400	Aircraft designer Gerard Vultee and his wife Sylvia were killed in a plane crash on nearby East Pocket Mesa in 1938.
Long Canyon (122)	FR 152D	3.0	500	Outstanding stands of Arizona cypress.
Boynton Canyon (47)	Near Boynton Canyon Ranch (John Gardiner's Enchantment)	2.5	440	Cliff dwellings
Fay Canyon Arch (53)	FR 152C	0.8	240	Sinagua ruin under arch, western soapberry trees, Emory oaks.
Loy Canyon (5)	Near north end of FR 525	5.0	1680	Built by Samuel Loy family, 1880s, to move livestock back and forth from the Woody Mountain area near Flagstaff. The Loys lived here to escape malaria prevalent along the Verde River at the time.
Secret Mountain (109)	North end of Loy Canyon Trail	3.0	200	
Mooney Canyon (12)	FR 525C	4.5	1400	Mooney was a pioneer stockman; javelina common here.
Casner Mountain (8)	FR 525C	7.0	2100	George R. Casner pastured sheep here around 1900.
Dogie (116)	FR 525C	6.0 (to FT 63)	500	Sycamore Pass entrance to Sycamore Canyon Wilderness Area.

RED ROCK SOUTH MAP

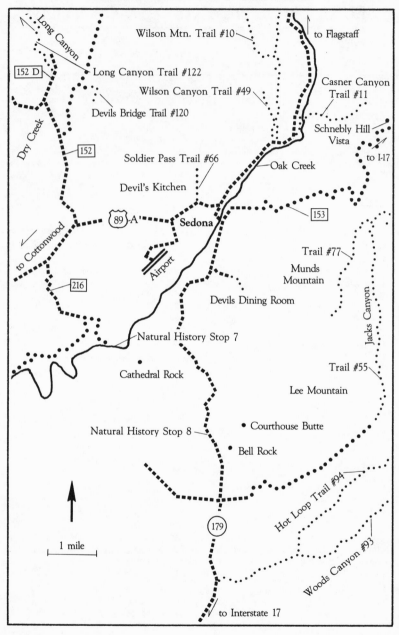

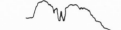

CHAPTER 3

RED ROCK SOUTH

I knew nothing of psychic forces, vortexes and the like when I first traveled to Sedona in 1973. I was a tourist, an avid shopper and a weaver. I came down Oak Creek Canyon from Flagstaff—a thrilling drive of hairpin turns and sheer cliffs— and entered another world. Even then I felt drawn to the area. I was energized and cleansed in a way I didn't understand and I said later that Sedona had an atmosphere that couldn't be defined.
A testimonial from *Sedona: Psychic Energy Vortexes*, 1986.

In 1885, six days were required to go from a ranch on lower Oak Creek to Flagstaff via the Beaver Head Stage Station, a distance of fifty miles. But following the Homestead Act of 1862, a number of people moved into the Red Rock Country.

Many of the families living in the canyon built trails from the creek up to the rim to shorten the distance to Flagstaff. They would keep their wagons on top, moving only their draft animals up and down the trail.

In 1901 Oak Creek pioneer and teacher Daniel Ellsworth Schnebly encouraged his brother, T. Carl, to move to the mouth of Oak Creek Canyon. Eighty acres along the creek suitable for farming were for sale. Carl, his wife Sedona and their young children, Pearl and Ellsworth, arrived from Missouri on a freight car via the narrow gauge railroad to Jerome. They bounced their way in a wagon to the mouth of Oak Creek Canyon and lived in tents while building a house where the Los Abrigados Resort now stands.

In 1902, the Schneblys wanted to start a post office and applied with two names: Oak Creek Crossing and Schnebly Station. The postal authorities in Washington, D.C. declared both names too long for a cancellation stamp. Ellsworth suggested his twenty-five-year-old sister-in-law's name, Sedona, and on July 26, 1902 her name became the official name of the community.

The old Munds Trail, begun in the 1890s, eventually developed into the Verde Cut-Off, then Munds Road, and in 1904 became the Schnebly Hill Road. Located near the bottom of the new road, the Schnebly's two-story house was dubbed the Schnebly Resort Hotel. Here, weary travelers could find lodging and meals for a dollar a day. On Sundays, guests were treated to rich custards and chicken with noodles while Sedona played the piano.

From the town of Sedona south to Interstate 17 there is a beautiful drive through rolling red hills covered with pinyon pine-juniper woodland and interspersed with open parks of desert grassland. Numerous buttes and mesas punctuate the scene.

Start your trip meter at the junction of Highways 179 and 89A. About 1.3 miles south on **State Highway 179** you will come to **Morgan Road** (MP 312.1) which leads into the Broken Arrow Estates. Morgan Road ends in a half mile and unless you have a four-wheel drive, you will have to walk another half mile to reach the **Devil's Dining Room**, a seventy-five-foot-deep sinkhole, one of several in the Sedona area. Sinkholes usually

Globemallow

form when the roof of a limestone cavern collapses. But these openings are in the Schnebly Hill Formation which is mainly sandstone. Perhaps they are related to some feature in a deeply buried limestone layer. Notice that a volcanic dike cuts through one of the walls of the sink.

Back on the highway, another 1.5 miles brings you to **Little Horse Park.** In February 1987, the Arizona State Transportation Board designated the seven-and-one-half miles of Highway 179 from Little Horse Park through the Village of Oak Creek to within three miles of Interstate 17 as the Red Rock Scenic Road. "Scenic Road" status provides that the Arizona Department of Transportation, in cooperation with local governments, will take measures to preserve and enhance highways which traverse especially scenic and historic parts of the state.

Another 2.3 miles and you are at the **Bell Rock Vista Point** turn-out on the right (MP 308.3). This is Natural History Stop 8.

Natural History Stop 8
BELL ROCK VISTA POINT

Elevation: 4360 feet   Milepost 308.3

The Liberty Bell-shaped Bell Rock was one of the sites for the August, 1987 Harmonic Convergence—believed by some to be a time when the planets were aligned in a special way that would mark a new age for mankind. Whether or not you believe in such things, the beauty of this spot is a commanding force.

The upper faces and steep slickrock slopes of Bell Rock and Court-house Rock (oldtimers insist that the proper name for this monolith is Cathedral Rock) are made of Schnebly Hill Sandstone. The lower slopes are Hermit Shale. To the northeast, Munds Mountain can be seen to be disconnected from Lee Mountain by a fault. Notice the displacement of similar rock layers on either side of the fault line.

Vegetation within this pinyon pine-juniper woodland is much more diverse than it appears at first glance. Sugar sumac, manzanita, Arizona cypress, narrowleaf yucca, banana yucca, Parry's agave, shrub live oak, catclaw acacia, prickly pear, and a host of wildflowers are found here after the summer rains begin.

Most of the area across the road, including Bell Rock, Courthouse Rock, Munds Mountain and Lee Mountain, lies within the new Munds Mountain Wilderness Area designated in 1984.

Continue past Bell Rock and you enter **Big Park**, now the site of the **Village of Oak Creek**. From this point south, the red rocks quickly disappear underground due to faulting or because they are buried by lavas and ancient river gravels.

The washes or dry arroyos cutting through the flatness of the park are the result of recent erosion. Not only has the physical landscape changed through time, but the plant, animal, and human communities have also continually evolved. Two million years ago, the climate of the Red Rock Country was much wetter and cooler than it is today. Fossil remnants of the stegomastodon, an intermediate form between the more primitive mastodon and the modern elephant, a small three-toed horse, camel, giant condor, Dirk-toothed cat, jaguar, a species of horse similar to the Polish horse, and llama have been found in the Verde Valley and Red Rock

Ice Age Scene—Stegomastodon at Red Rock Crossing

Country area. These now extinct creatures roamed the Red Rock Country during the Pleistocene.

Some of the Pleistocene fauna evolved into new forms while others became extinct. Over much of the southwest, many extinctions seem to coincide with the arrival of the first humans on the scene. (Note: So far there is no conclusive evidence of paleo-Indian hunters in the Red Rock Country from 9500 B.C. to 8500 B.C.; yet the same Pleistocene species disappeared here, too.) Some archaeologists argue that these early hunters hastened along the extinction of these great beasts that were already having difficulty adapting to a warming and drying environment.

The vegetation was one of the first biotic features to change. Desert-adapted plants from the south and from arid regions to the north merged to form a fairly unique chaparral plant community along the Mogollon Rim. Pinyon pine and juniper woodlands expanded into former grasslands. A few of the "Ice Age" species were able to tolerate or adapt to the new conditions and survived.

Within historic times, there have been additional dramatic changes. Prior to the 1890s, the Verde River was a slow, shallow stream reportedly containing "clumps of grass" (probably sedges and rushes). Early pioneer accounts describe the river banks as spongy and water-logged, ideal for mosquito breeding. Malaria was common and accounted for more fatalities than Indians or outlaws. Cutting of the streamside trees and overgrazing by sheep, horses and cattle stripped away the vegetation, dried the ground, and increased the erosive powers of flash floods. Changes in the rainfall pattern also occurred. Deep "arroyos" or washes were cut. Cheat grass, tumbleweed, snakeweed, rabbitbrush, and other unpalatable plants invaded the grazing land, a sad but common story over much of the Southwest.

Evolve, adapt, or perish are the rules of nature's game. In the last ten thousand years or so, there has been a slow drying and warming trend in the climate of the Southwest. Some species have been able to adapt to the new conditions while others moved to higher and generally wetter, cooler habitats. Their geographic distribution may have become spotty or disjunct, resulting in relatively isolated populations. Others became extinct.

In the Red Rock Country there are a number of plants and animals that are now "stranded" as disjunct populations or relicts of past conditions. Examples include: red osier dogwood, osha, Gambel oak (perhaps an evolutionary split off the eastern white oak), Douglas fir, white fir, bigtooth maple, Arizona cypress, and hophornbeam. The narrow-headed

Narrow-headed gartersnake

gartersnake, Arizona gray squirrel, desert-grassland whiptail lizard, Arizona treefrog and southwestern toad definitely occur in disjunct populations and may be animal relicts.

Several plants may have evolved in central Arizona and are considered endemic to the area. Arizona bugbane, mock-pennyroyal, Arizona groundsel, and the fleabane, *Erigeron pringlei*, are four such species generally limited to the Mogollon Rim and the central Arizona mountains, including Oak Creek. Distribution of endemics is often limited by very specific habitat requirements for the organism. For example, the mock-pennyroyal will only grow in slight depressions within dolomitic limestone (limestone high in magnesium) and a thirty to thirty-five percent "canopy" or tree cover.

Some botanists consider the cypress, *Cupressus glabra*, growing along Oak Creek and the Mogollon Rim a distinct species, and therefore endemic, but there is much disagreement about some plant classifications. One endemic animal is the Page Springs snail (*Pyrgulopsis morrisoni*) which is only found in the Verde Valley area and especially near Page Springs on lower Oak Creek.

Some organisms can be considered special because of their rarity despite widespread geographic distribution. The endangered peregrine falcon and the shy spotted owl both can be found in the Oak Creek Canyon area, but it is unlikely the casual visitor will see one of these magnificent birds.

Unfortunately, several animals are noteworthy because of their extirpation through overhunting. The grizzly bear, Merriam's elk, and bighorn sheep were all eliminated from the area by the early 1900s.

Near the south end of the Village, **Jack's Canyon Road** (FR 793, MP 306.2) takes off to the left (east). Follow it not quite three miles to the Pine Valley development. Immediately before entering private land, **Jack's Canyon Trail** (named after Jack Woods, a railroad engineer from Winslow who grazed sheep in this area in the 1880s) a main entry into the 18,150-acre **Munds Mountain Wilderness Area**, is on the right. This 6.5 mile trail will take you to a saddle between Munds Mountain and the Schnebly Hill. The Munds Mountain Trail goes from the saddle to the top of the mountain.

As you continue south, the road subtly loses elevation. Pinyons disappear and one-seed juniper becomes dominant. Catclaw acacia, narrowleaf yucca, and mesquite are more common. Along the roadside are snakeweed, purple nightshade, dock, and prickly pear cactus. About two miles south of Jack's Canyon Road is the turnoff for **Woods Canyon** and **Hot Loop Trails** (MP 304.8). Cross the **Dry Beaver Creek** bridge (MP 302.5) (there is sometimes a roaring torrent in the spring) and drive almost a mile. Turn right at the historical marker sign (MP 301.6), go through the gate and take the turn to the right. The marker is located about a tenth of a mile inside the fence and designates the location of the **Beaver Head Stage Station**, built in 1876 and abandoned six years later. This station was located on the old Stoneman Road which was carved out in 1867 and became Arizona's second major wagon road. (The number one road crossing northern Arizona was Beale's Road which later became the famous Highway Route 66.)

Continue three miles down Highway 179 to Interstate 17.

Hophornbeam

TRAIL CHART FOR RED ROCK SOUTH

Name (USFS Trail #)	Trailhead Location	Length (one-way miles)	Climb (feet)	Features
Devil's Dining Room	MP 312.1	0.5	80	Sinkhole 75 feet deep, 25 feet across; contains a volcanic dike.
Jack's Canyon (55)	MP 306.2	6.5	2000	Cattle trail built 1882-1884 by C.M. (Jack) Montgomery, Al Doyle and John Marshall.
Munds Mountain (77)	Head of Jack's Canyon	2.5	450	Great views of the Red Rock Country.
Hot Loop (94)	MP 304.8	4.0	1200	
Woods Canyon (93)	MP 304.8	14.0 (to I17)	1260	Only about 3 miles of trail, the rest is boulder hopping.

Spotted skunk

CHAPTER 4

NEARBY ATTRACTIONS

NORTH ON U.S. HIGHWAY 89A

U.S. Highway 89A north from Oak Creek leads to historic **Flagstaff,** beautifully situated at the southern base of the San Francisco Peaks. The **San Francisco Mountain Volcanic Field** is comprised of some 400 cinder cones and volcanoes and is one of the largest volcanic areas in the United States. Astronauts slated for lunar missions train here because of its moon-like appearance. **Sunset Crater National Monument** includes a very young lava flow (a mere 900 years old) as well as other dramatic volcanic features.

I recommend that you begin your exploration of the natural and human history of the area with a visit to the **Museum of Northern Arizona.** The Arizona Historical Society **Pioneer Museum** and **Riordan State Historic Park** are also highly recommended for the history buff. For those interested in the ancient Sinagua, **Walnut Canyon National Monument, Wupatki National Monument,** and **Elden Pueblo** are excellent sites.

The Lowell Observatory and the Coconino Center for the Arts are also very interesting places to visit.

Hikers can climb the highest peak in Arizona in the **Kachina Peaks Wilderness Area** or explore the forest around the **Kendrick Mountain Wilderness**. During the winter months, downhill skiers enjoy the slopes at the **Fairfield Snowbowl** while cross-country enthusiasts kick and glide along snow-covered roads traversing the **Coconino National Forest.**

Within a few hours of Flagstaff there are still more attractions, including the world-famous **Grand Canyon National Park, Petrified Forest National Park, Meteor Crater,** and the **Navajo** and **Hopi Indian Reservations.**

Hooded Oriole

SOUTHWEST ON U.S. HIGHWAY 89A

Southwest from Oak Creek on U.S. Highway 89A, the town of **Jerome** is perched precariously on the side of Cleopatra Hill. Jerome was once Arizona Territory's third largest city. Only about 400 residents call the old copper mining town home today, but visitors can find delightful restaurants and shops while gazing out across the Verde Valley to the Red Rock Country. Jerome's colorful past is brought to life at the Jerome State Historic Park and the Jerome Historical Society's Mine Museum. **Dead Horse Ranch State Park,** located on the Verde River, is a paradise for birders in late spring and early summer. On lower Oak Creek, wintering bald eagles are often seen at the **Page Springs Fish Hatchery.**

At **Tuzigoot National Monument,** one of the great hilltop communal cities erected along the Verde by the Sinagua is preserved.

For the backpacker, the 55,942-acre **Sycamore Canyon Wilderness Area** offers country similar to Oak Creek Canyon but without the cars and crowds.

SOUTH ON STATE 179 AND INTERSTATE 17

To discover the special features of the Verde Valley, start at the Montezuma Castle-Yavapai/Apache Tribal Visitor Center just off Interstate 17 on the Camp Verde exit.

Montezuma Castle and **Montezuma Well National Monuments** near Camp Verde contain excellent examples of Sinagua pueblos and cliff dwellings. Early white settlers believed that Aztecs had built the many ruins found in the Verde Valley, but Montezuma, leader of the Aztecs in Mexico, had no connection with either of these areas.

Fort Verde State Historic Park is located in the town of **Camp Verde**. The Fort, built from 1871 to 1873, is the third fort to occupy this site. This fort was never attacked and was never enclosed by a wall. It served as a supply base and staging area for army operations and was finally abandoned in 1891.

Nearby the **Beaver Creek** and **West Clear Creek Wilderness Areas** beckon backcountry explorers.

The drive from Sedona to the desert metropolis of Phoenix takes about two hours.

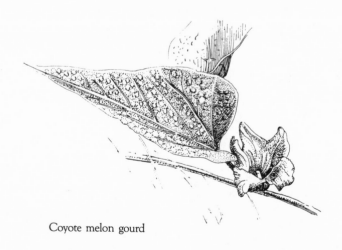

Coyote melon gourd

Moonrise at Cathedral Rock—Tom Bean photo

Sedona nestles at the mouth of Oak Creek Canyon; San Francisco Peaks in background—Stewart Aitchison

View from above Secret Canyon—Tom Bean

The Mogollon Rim and Red Rock Country northwest of Sedona; San Francisco Peaks in background—Stewart Aitchison

Devil's Bridge was caused by erosion along joints—Stewart Aitchison

Oak Creek Canyon from Overlook (Natural History Stop 1)— Stewart Aitchison

Cardinal flower (*Lobelia cardinalis*)—Stewart Aitchison

Late afternoon view from Schnebly Hill Road—Stewart Aitchison

A winter day at Midgley Bridge—Stewart Aitchison

Snow-covered red rock near Midgley Bridge—Martos Hoffman

West Fork—Stewart Aitchison

Sinagua cliff dwelling in the Red Rock Country—Charles Bame

Prehistoric pictograph of a flute player in the Red Rock Country—Stewart Aitchison

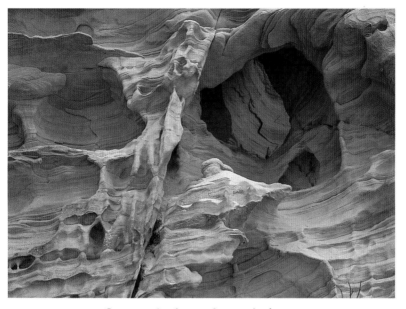

Coconino Sandstone—Stewart Aitchison

Slide Rock State Park (Natural History Stop 3)—Stewart Aitchison

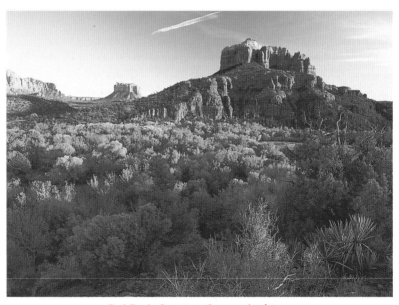

Red Rock Crossing—Stewart Aitchison

Autumn near Midgley Bridge—Stewart Aitchison

Fruit of the prickly pear cactus—Stewart Aitchison

Rainbow at Red Rock Crossing—Tom Bean

Bear Mountain rises abruptly from Hartwell Canyon—Tom Bean

Dry Creek vista (Natural History Stop 6)—Stewart Aitchison

Natural History Stop 6

—Some of the plants at this stop include prickly pear cactus, manzanita, pinyon pine, banana yucca

—Stewart Aitchison

Agave at Bell Rock Vista (Natural History Stop 8)—Stewart Aitchison

Chapel of the Holy Cross south of Sedona—Stewart Aitchison

Sycamore Canyon Wilderness Area—Stewart Aitchison

Sunset at Cathedral Rock—Tom Bean

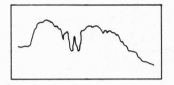

PART II
Ready Reference

ORIGIN OF THE ROCKS

Geologic Cross-section

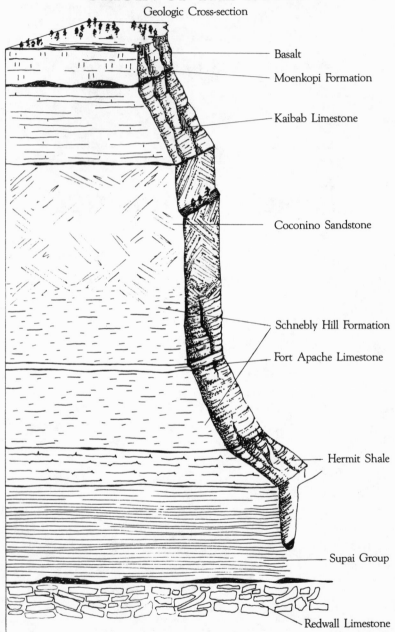

Basalt

Moenkopi Formation

Kaibab Limestone

Coconino Sandstone

Schnebly Hill Formation

Fort Apache Limestone

Hermit Shale

Supai Group

Redwall Limestone

□

ORIGIN OF THE ROCKS

□

Basalt Cap, 0–600 feet. Forms cliffs.
Tertiary (5–8 million years old)
   Composed of dark gray lavas. Often cooled and fractured by columnar jointing. Individual flows often separated by reddish-orange layers of "baked" soil.

Moenkopi Formation, 0–60 feet. Forms slopes and ledges.
Triassic (225 million years old)
   Composed of red sandstones, siltstones, and shales. Only erosional remnants remain of what used to cover most of the Red Rock Country. Fossil ripple marks indicate that flowing water was common.

Kaibab Limestone, 100–400 feet. Forms cliffs and ledges.
Middle Permian (250 million years old)
   Composed of a sandy, whitish to tan limestone. Contains "vugs" or dissolved cavities filled with dog-tooth calcite or silica. Pink to yellow globs of chert are common. The molds of mollusks, brachiopods, and gastropods including *Archaeocidaris, Plagioglypta,* and *Eucomphalus* are sometimes found along with fossilized burrows. The imprints of sponges are common. These fossils indicate that this rock layer was deposited in a warm, near-shore marine environment.

Coconino Sandstone, 700 feet. Forms cliffs.
Early Permian (270 million years old)
   Composed of buff to cream-colored sand, deposited as eolian (windblown) dunes, now preserved as crossbedded sandstone. Small reptile tracks are common, although no fossils of the animals have been discovered. Curiously, the fossil tracks usually go only up bedding planes; downhill tracks apparently were destroyed as the animal descended the soft sand. In Oak Creek Canyon, the Coconino tends to exhibit massive, distinctive crossbedding in its lower cliff separated from the higher portion of the cliff by a small bench usually covered with vegetation. The upper cliff exhibits eolian as well as shallow marine characteristics and thus has been called a separate formation (Toroweap) by some geologists.

Schnebly Hill Formation, 750–800 feet. Forms cliffs and steep slopes.
Early Permian (275 million years old)

Composed of grayish-orange to reddish-brown fine-grained sandstone.
About mid-way down the Schnebly Hill Formation is the gray to purplish
Fort Apache Limestone (10–30 feet) which is believed to be a brief incur-
sion of a shallow sea. The limestone is more resistant to erosion than the
sandstone, so it often forms a ledge or bench such as at Merry-go-round
Rock along Schnebly Hill Road.

The Schnebly Hill Formation contains only a few fossil burrows; no
other fossils have been found. In the Fort Apache Limestone just east
of the Red Rock Country, fragments of mollusks and echinoderms have
been found. Geologic evidence suggests that these formations were
deposited in a warm, very salty, tidal flat. To the north was a vast dune
desert (the Coconino Sandstone) which eventually encroached upon this
area.

Hermit Shale, 200 feet. Forms slopes.
Early Permian (280 million years old)

Composed of purplish-red limey sandstones and siltstone. Fern-like
impressions, molds of the Paleozoic conifer *Lebachia piniformis*, stromatolite
(algae) mounds, burrows, and highly oxidized iron particles suggest a shallow
swamp to tidal environment during this time.

Supai Group, 500 feet.
Pennsylvanian/Permian (300 million years old)

Composed of red to pink siltstone and sandstone. Forms the "inner
gorge" which begins near the mouth of Casner Canyon and runs
downstream to Sedona.

Redwall Limestone, unknown thickness. Forms cliffs.
Early-Middle Mississippian (330 million years old)

Composed of gray limestone, the Redwall received its name in the Grand
Canyon where the overlying red formations have stained the limestone.
Although not exposed within Oak Creek Canyon, it does outcrop in lower
Dry Creek and the mouth of Sycamore Canyon; it underlies the Red Rock
Country. Earlier reports of Redwall Limestone in Oak Creek Canyon are
now considered limey sections of the Supai Group.

A Brief 330-Million-Year History of the Red Rock Country

Years Ago

330 million -	A thick layer of nearly pure limestone is deposited in the warm Redwall Sea.
330–300	Uplifting of the area exposed the Redwall Limestone to erosion followed by subsidence and the invasion of sluggish rivers carrying silt, mud, and sand that deposited the Supai Group.
300–280	After a period of erosion, the region became a vast floodplain within a semiarid area. Rivers draining from the north and east deposited thick layers of mud to form the Hermit Shale.
280–275	The land subsided a little more and the area became a tidal flat where the Schnebly Hill sands are laid down. At one point the sea briefly invaded to deposit the Fort Apache Limestone.
275–270	The Coconino dune desert to the north invaded the tidal flat. For five million years, the Red Rock Country was covered by shifting dunes hundreds of feet thick.
270–250	The land subsided once again and the Kaibab Sea encroached. Mollusks, brachiopods, gastropods, trilobites, and sponges inhabited this warm, shallow sea. The calcareous body parts of marine creatures accumulateed into limestone.
250–225	Another uplift, the sea retreated and the area became a low coastal plain where rivers deposited mud, silt, and sand to form the Moenkopi.
225–65	Other sedimentary rock layers were deposited.
65–15	Uplifting and erosion erased upper rock layers down to the Permian Age (Kaibab Limestone) from the Red Rock Country except for remnants of the Moenkopi Formation.
15–present	Volcanic activity, lava flows, continued faulting, uplift, and erosion of present canyons.

OAKS OF OAK CREEK

Oak Creek Canyon couldn't be more appropriately named. An 1879 map of the Arizona Territory shows the stream designated as "Live Oak Creek," a reference to the ubiquitous evergreen oaks found throughout the canyon. There are about nine species of oak found in the Red Rock Country. I say "about" nine because the exact number depends upon whether you are a "splitter" or a "lumper," two general groups of scientists who study and attempt to name and classify natural phenomena. The splitters look for every opportunity to separate out what they consider to be distinct species, while the lumpers try to combine similar plants or creatures under one name. (Indeed, this business of taxonomy is a bit artificial and something to which the vegetation and wildlife pay no heed.)

But back to the oaks. The oaks often interbreed, producing hybrid forms that don't fit the taxonomist's list. Most botanists would agree that in Oak Creek there are Gambel oaks (*Quercus gambelii*), a deciduous oak, usually ten to forty feet tall (though it may be short and shrubby). It is commonly scattered throughout the pine forest and extends into the canyon where sufficient water and cooler temperatures are found. Its large, deeply-lobed leaves are bigger than any other of the southwestern oaks. In many ways, Gambel oak resembles a stunted, crooked white oak (*Q. alba*) and may some day be regarded as a variety of that eastern species, split off from its ancesters by an accident of Pleistocene biogeography. The wood of the Gambel oak is used for fence posts and is prized by locals as firewood. This oak and the Gambel quail are named after William Gambel, a Philadelphia physician, ornithologist, and botanist who passed through Santa Fe, New Mexico, in 1841 on his way to California. Gambel discovered a hundred new plant species during the expedition.

The shrub live oak (*Q. turbinella*), sometimes called scrub oak, is also found in the canyon. This evergreen oak is common on hot, dry slopes and is an important component of the chaparral community. It usually grows as a shrub less than eight feet tall but occasionally reaches to fifteen feet as a tree with an open, spreading crown. While this species and other southwestern oaks provide browse for deer and livestock, tannin poison-

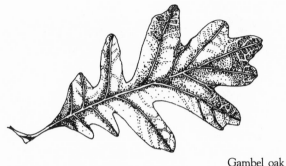

Gambel oak

ing may occur in livestock if more than three-fourths of their diet consists of oak foliage. The acorns are an important food for Steller jays,
band-tailed pigeons, turkeys, and squirrels.

Arizona white oak (*Q. arizonica*) is the largest of the evergreen oaks
in the Red Rock Country, growing thirty to sixty feet tall. Its bark is fissured
into thick, light gray or whitish plates. The leaves are oblong, one to three
inches long, thick and stiff, only slightly toothed, dull blue-green with
sunken veins above; they are paler and densely hairy with prominent raised
veins on the underside. This oak can be seen along Dry Beaver Creek
in Wood's Canyon.

Canyon live oak (*Q. chrysolepis*) is considered by the lumpers to be
Palmer oak (*Q. c. var. palmeri*). It is an evergreen oak six to twenty-five
feet tall with thick, leathery leaves that are glossy green above and golden-
yellow below due to tiny yellow hairs. The leaf margin may be smooth
or spiny-toothed.

Palmer oak (*Q. dunnii* or *Q. palmeri*) is named after Edward Palmer,
an American botanical collector who explored Mexico and the Southwest
in the late 1800s. One authority separates this species from *Q. chrysolepis*
on the grounds that it is "usually" a shrub while the latter is "usually"
a tree. Look for canyon live and Palmer oaks in the Dry Creek area.

Emory oak (*Q. emoryi*) is named after Lt. Col. William H. Emory, leader
of an 1846–47 military expedition to the Southwest during the Mexican
War and a boundary survey party a few years later. This oak prefers moist
places, especially in the canyons. Its acorns are nearly free of bitter-tasting
tannin and were gathered and eaten by Indians. Its black bark has led

to its other common name: black oak. There are some nice specimens of this oak in Fay Canyon.

Gray oak (*Q. grisea*) interbreeds freely with Arizona white oak and shrub live oak and therefore can be difficult to identify. A "purebred" tends to be a low shrub with elliptical leaves three-quarters of an inch to two inches long, slightly heart-shaped at the base, edges without teeth or with a few teeth toward the apex, gray-green, shiny and sparsely-haired above, densely-haired beneath. It is occasionally found among pinyon and juniper.

Netleaf oak (*Q. reticulata*) is an uncommon small tree or shrub. The yellow hairy underside of the leaf has a network of raised veins.

Wavyleaf oak (*Q. undulata*) is a low shrubby resident of the dry slopes and occurs often on burned areas. Its leaves are usually wavy and lobed.

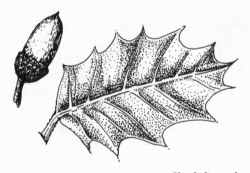

Shrub live oak

THE LAST 65,000,000 YEARS

The Making of Today's Landscape

The last sixty-five million years of geologic history in Oak Creek Canyon is quite complex and is still not completely understood. The following diagrams present a very simplified "big picture" as generally agreed upon today.

Million of Years Ago (Dates are approximate)

65–30   Mogollon Highlands, to the south of what will later become the Red Rock Country, drain across a plain to the north onto the ancestral Colorado Plateau region. Late Mesozoic and early Cenozoic (140 to 40 mya) rock layers are removed by erosion.

50   Initial movement along Oak Creek Fault begins to lift east block up relative to west block. Erosion begins to remove the rock layers on top of the higher eastern block faster than the lower west block. Certain sections of the Mogollon Rim begin to form.

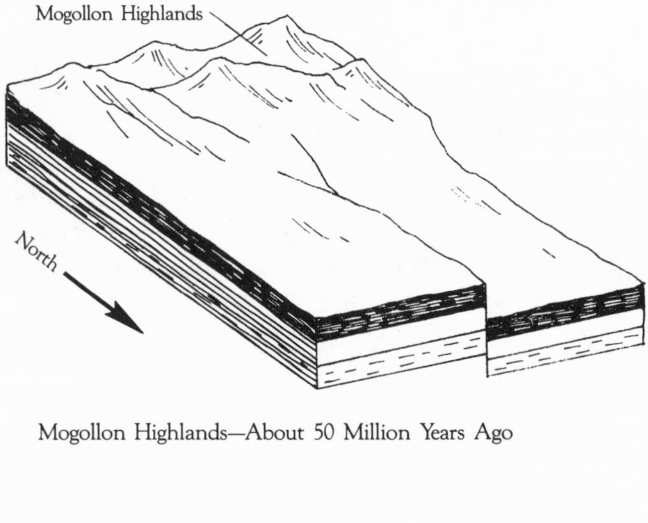

Mogollon Highlands—About 50 Million Years Ago

15–10   Major period of faulting begins. The Black Hills to the southwest of the Sedona area are uplifted. Drainage of area reverses to a north-to-south pattern as Mogollon Rim forming the southern edge of the Colorado Plateau becomes a more well-defined structural feature.

8–5   More faulting, which results in the damming of the ancestral Verde River and the formation of a series of lakes. Along the Mogollon Rim above Oak Creek Fault at least seven periods of eruptions result in basalt flows totaling up to 600 feet in thickness. The basalt caps erosional remnants of the Moenkopi Formation, the Kaibab Limestone of the West Block and the Coconino Sandstone surface of the now severely eroded East Block. Some flows are from vents near Woody Mountain.

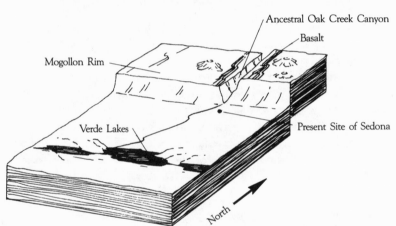

Ancestral Oak Creek Canyon

Basalt

Mogollon Rim

Verde Lakes

Present Site of Sedona

North

Initial Oak Creek Fault Movement—About 7 Million Years Ago

5   A second period of faulting along Oak Creek Fault drops the eastern block more than 700 feet relative to the western block. More basalt flows occur. Headward erosion along faults and joints establishes the Oak Creek and Dry Creek drainages and their tributaries. One of the Verde Lakes reaches the 4300-foot contour in the Dry Creek drainage.

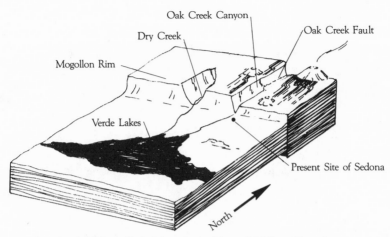

Second Major Fault Movement—About 5 Million Years Ago

1.6   A channel is worn by the Verde River through the mountains at the southeast end of the Valley and the Verde Lakes drain. Erosion continues to deepen and widen canyons. Difference in width between Oak Creek Canyon and Dry Creek is due to the Oak Creek Rim being protected by a hard basalt cap. There is no such cap near Dry Creek and the forces of erosion can act more quickly on the relatively soft sedimentary stone. Continued widening of joints isolates mesas which through time are eroded to buttes, then reduced to pinnacles.

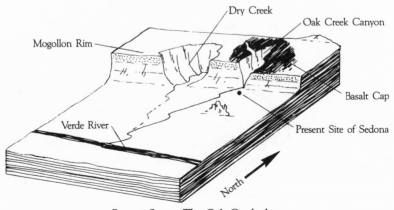

Present Scene—The Oak Creek Area

□

HISTORICAL HIGHLIGHTS

□

Date	Event
2000 B.C.-0 A.D.	Archaic Period (6000 B.C.-0 A.D.) people pass through area in search of game and wild plant foods.
0-700	Sinagua living in shallow pithouses, no pottery; growing corn marks the beginning of agriculture.
700-1000	Hohokam influence becomes noticeable.
1000-1130	Sinagua consolidate into villages.
1130-1300	Uplands largely abandoned in favor of river valley occupation; small, scattered pueblos combine to form forty large pueblos and cliff houses, mostly near rivers and streams (e.g. Honanki near Loy Butte).
1300-1400	Great hilltop pueblos, such as Tuzigoot along the Verde River, reach their zenith.
1400-1425	For reasons not fully understood, the Sinagua leave area. (Or they may have become the Yavapai.)
1400-mid-1800s	Northeast Yavapai and Tonto Apache hunting and gathering; left mescal roasting pits, wickiup outlines, pictographs, small sherd and lithic scatters. They moved seasonally following wild game and water supply.
1583	Led by Hopis, Antonio de Espejo enters Verde Valley probably via an Indian trail that descends Wet Beaver Creek some twenty miles southeast of Oak Creek. He is ostensibly looking for two friars but is probably more interested in prospecting. He is disappointed to discover that Indian mines in the valley are copper rather than gold or silver. Espejo is the first Euro-American in the Verde Valley and the first to contact the Yavapai.
1598	Marcos Farfan de los Godos expedition encounters Cruzados—"people with crosses" (Yavapai)—a name that persisted until 1716.
1605	Yavapai trade with Hopi is noted by Escobar.

1849	Whipple refers to Yampaio (Yavapai) on Colorado River, later confused with Apache.
1854	Trapper and guide Antoine Leroux discovers ruins of Verde Valley.
1857–58	Road laid out from Winslow to Prescott.
1860–70s	Pioneers settle in Verde Valley; Yavapai-Apaches are forcibly moved out of Valley to San Carlos Reservation.
1863	Captain Joseph Walker, while prospecting, may be the first Anglo-American in the Red Rock area.
1865	Camp Verde is settled.
1870	C.S. "Bear" Howard settles at the mouth of West Fork.
1872	General Crook begins an offensive action against Apaches.
1873	Yavapai-Apache wars are concluded.
1876	John Jim Thompson settles at Indian Gardens and becomes the first Anglo settler in Oak Creek. Beaver Head Stage Station becomes a stop on the Prescott to Albuquerque road.
1878	Abraham James family becomes first to live in Sedona area.
1880s	Devil's Kitchen forms with a crash; Camp Verde officers have a summer camp (Camp Garden) in Grasshopper Flat; first wagon goes from Sedona area to Cottonwood.
1882	First Anglo child born in Sedona area—James Frank to Jim and Maggie Thompson.
1885	Richard Wilson is killed by a bear in Wilson Canyon.
1887	Jim Thompson's early road from Sedona to Indian Gardens washes out and he builds a higher one around the base of Steamboat Rock.
1896	John Loy improves Munds Trail from Sedona to Bear Wallow Canyon into a road.
1899	Archaeologist Jesse Walter Fewkes predicts future popularity of the Red Rock Country. First Oak Creek Campground; open summers only.
1900–1906	Lou Thomas builds road from Flagstaff to West Fork.
1901	Wagon road completed from Sedona to Indian Gardens.
1902	Sedona Post Office is established; Oak Creek school is moved to Indian Gardens; Schnebly Hill Road is begun with county funds.
1903	Big flood washes out part of Mormon Camp located at the mouth of Mormon Canyon near the north end of Sedona.

It was a popular fishing spot and was as far up Oak Creek Canyon as a wagon could be driven in the 1880s.

1904 Schnebly Hill Road is completed.

1905 William Wallace becomes the first forest ranger of the Sedona Ranger District.

1909 Big flood washes away rest of Mormon Camp.

1910 First Sedona School is constructed.

1914 First wagon road through Oak Creek Canyon is finished and crosses creek 16 times; first bridge across Oak Creek at Oak Creek Falls is erected.

1917 John Jim Thompson dies.

1918 Big flood takes out Oak Creek Falls Bridge.

1923 Hollywood discovers Sedona and Oak Creek; "Call of the Canyon" is filmed in canyon.

1924 Tunnel south of Encinoso is eliminated.

1930 Schnebly Hill Road is re-engineered; most of the original route is abandoned.

1932 "Riders of the Purple Sage" is filmed in the area; there are many CCC and WPA projects, including road work and trail construction.

1936 Electricity comes to Sedona.

1938 Big flood on March 3rd takes out second Oak Creek Falls Bridge.

1939 Midgley Bridge is dedicated and the road through Oak Creek Canyon is paved.

1940s First telephone comes to Sedona, a Forest Service line.

1944–1959 An average of two motion pictures per year are filmed in the area.

1949 Forest Service withdraws Oak Creek Canyon from mineral entry, establishing the canyon as a Scenic Area; electricity reaches upper Oak Creek Canyon.

1950 Sedona Schnebly dies.

1954 T.C. Schnebly dies; first local telephone exchange installed.

1955 Forest Service makes further mineral withdrawals adding to the Scenic Area.

1956 Chapel of the Holy Cross is designed by sculptress Marguerite Brunswig Staude as a memorial to her parents.

1966 Sedona Airport is established.

1978 Sedona's population is 4400 residents.

1984	Red Rock-Secret Mountain Wilderness and Munds Mountain Wilderness areas are designated.
1986	Oak Creek Canyon has 2.5 million visitors.
1987	Slide Rock State Park opens; Sedona incorporates with about 8500 residents.

Arizona bugbane

BREEDING BIRDS OF OAK CREEK CANYON

A Partial List

Peregrine Falcon
Band-tailed Pigeon
Mourning Dove
White-throated Swift
Broad-tailed Hummingbird
Northern (Red-shafted) Flicker
Hairy Woodpecker
Black Phoebe
Western Wood Pewee
Violet-green Swallow
Northern Rough-winged Swallow
Steller's Jay
Mountain Chickadee
Red-breasted Nuthatch
White-breasted Nuthatch
Pygmy Nuthatch
Brown Creeper
Canyon Wren
Bewick's Wren
House Wren
American Dipper

American Robin
Hermit Thrush
Western Bluebird
Solitary Vireo
Warbling Vireo
Virginia's Warbler
Yellow Warbler
Yellow-rumped (Audubon's) Warbler
Grace's Warbler
Painted Redstart
Red-faced Warbler
Northern (Bullock's) Oriole
Western Tanager
Hepatic Tanager
Black-headed Grosbeak
Rufous-sided Towhee
Song Sparrow
House Finch
Pine Siskin
Lesser Goldfinch
Dark-eyed (Gray-headed) Junco

Painted Redstart

□

BIRDS OF LOWER OAK CREEK

A Partial List

□

(* indicates birds that often nest in the riparian habitat)

*Pied-billed Grebe
*Great Blue Heron
*Green-backed Heron
*Black-crowned Night Heron
Canada Goose
Mallard
Cinnamon Teal
*Common Merganser
Turkey Vulture
Bald Eagle
Northern Harrier
*Sharp-shinned Hawk
*Cooper's Hawk
*Common Black Hawk
*Red-tailed Hawk
*American Kestrel (Sparrow Hawk)
*Gambel's Quail
*Killdeer
*Spotted Sandpiper
Band-tailed Pigeon
*Mourning Dove
*Yellow-billed Cuckoo
Greater Roadrunner
*Great Horned Owl
Common Nighthawk
White-throated Swift
*Black-chinned Hummingbird
Rufous Hummingbird
*Belted Kingfisher
*Gila Woodpecker
*Yellow-bellied "Red-naped" Sapsucker
*Ladder-backed Woodpecker
*Northern Flicker
*Black Phoebe
Say's Phoebe

Water Pipit
Crissal Thrasher
Cedar Waxwing
*Phainopepla
Loggerhead Shrike
*Bell's Vireo
*Solitary Vireo
Orange-crowned Warbler
*Lucy's Warbler
*Yellow Warbler
Yellow-rumped Warbler
*Common Yellowthroat
Wilson's Warbler
*Yellow-breasted Chat
*Summer Tanager
*Northern Cardinal
*Black-headed Grosbeak
*Blue Grosbeak
*Lazuli Bunting
Rufous-sided Towhee
Brown Towhee
*Abert's Towhee
*Chipping Sparrow
Brewer's Sparrow
Savannah Sparrow
*Song Sparrow
Lincoln's Sparrow
White-crowned Sparrow
Dark-eyed Junco
*Red-winged Blackbird
*Western Meadowlark
*Yellow-headed Blackbird
*Brewer's Blackbird
*Great-tailed Grackle
*Northern Mockingbird

*Cassin's Kingbird
*Western Kingbird
*Brown-crested Flycatcher
*Ash-throated Flycatcher
*Violet-green Swallow
*Northern Rough-winged Swallow
*Cliff Swallow
*Steller's Jay
 Scrub Jay
 Pinyon Jay
 Common Raven
 Mountain Chickadee
*Bridled Titmouse
*Plain Titmouse
 Verdin
 Bushtit
 Rock Wren
 Canyon Wren
*Bewick's Wren
 Marsh Wren
 Ruby-crowned Kinglet
 Western Bluebird
*Townsend's Solitaire
*Hermit Thrush
*American Robin

*Hooded Oriole
*Northern Oriole
*House Finch
 Pine Siskin
*Lesser Goldfinch
 American Goldfinch

Hairy Woodpecker

SCIENTIFIC NAMES

Plants and Animals Mentioned in Text

Plants
agave - *Agave parryi*
algae - over 500 species in Oak Creek
alligator juniper - *Juniperus deppeana*
alpine fir - *Abies lasiocarpa*
Apache plume - *Fallugia paradoxa*
Arizona alder - *Alnus oblongifolia*
Arizona black walnut - *Juglans major*
Arizona bugbane - *Cimicifuga arizonica*
Arizona cypress - *Cupressus arizonica*
Arizona groundsel - *Senecio arizonicus*
Arizona rose - *Rosa arizonica*
Arizona sycamore - *Platanus wrightii*
Arizona thistle - *Cirsium arizonicum*
Arizona white oak - *Quercus arizonica*
arroyo willow - *Salix lasiolepis*
aster - *Aster* spp.
banana yucca - *Yucca baccata*
barberry - *Berberis haematocarpa*
bee balm - *Monarda menthaefolia*
bigtooth maple - *Acer grandidentatum*
birchleaf buckthorn - *Rhamnus betulaefolia*
blackberry - *Rubus procerus*
bluebells - *Mertensia macdougalli*
blue dicks - *Dichelostemma pulchellum*
box elder - *Acer negundo*
braken fern - *Pteridium aquilinum*
buckbrush - *Ceanothus* spp.
bugbane - *Cimicifuga arizonica*
canotia - *Canotia holacantha*
canyon live oak - *Quercus chrysolepis*
cardinal flower - *Lobelia cardinalis*
catclaw acacia - *Acacia greggii*
ceanothus - *Ceanothus* spp.

cheat grass - *Bromus tectorum*
claret-cup hedgehog cactus - *Echinocereus fasciculatus*
cliffrose - *Cowania mexicana*
columbine - *Aquilegia chrysantha*
coyote melon gourd - *Cucurbita foetidissima*
deerbrush ceanothus - *Ceanothus integerrimus*
desert ash - *Fraxinus anomala*
dock - *Rumex* spp.
Douglas fir - *Pseudotsuga menziesii*
elderberry - *Sambucus glauca*
Emory oak - *Quercus emoryi*
Engelmann spruce - *Picea engelmannii*
evening-primrose - *Oenothera* spp.
false paloverde - *Canotia holacantha*
flax - *Linum* spp.
fleabane - *Erigeron* spp.
fleabane (candidate for endangered species) - *Erigeron pringlei*
Fremont cottonwood - *Populus fremontii*
Gambel oak - *Quercus gambelii*
geranium - *Geranium* spp.
globemallow - *Sphaeralcea* spp.
goldeneye - *Viguiera* spp.
golden pea - *Thermopsis pinetorum*
goldenrod - *Solidago* spp.
gray oak - *Quercus grisea*
hackberry - *Celtis reticulata*
heron bill - *Erodium texanum*
hophornbeam - *Ostrya knowltoni*
horsetail rush - *Equisetum* spp.
Indian paintbrush - *Castilleja* spp.
jimson weed -*Datura meteloides*

larkspur - *Delphinium geranifolium*
lousewort - *Pedicularis centranthera*
Lowell ash - *Fraxinus anomala* var.
   lowellii
lupine - *Lupinus* spp.
manzanita - *Arctostaphylos* spp.
meadowrue - *Thalictrum fendleri*
mesquite - *Prosopis juliflora*
mock-pennyroyal - *Hedeoma diffusum*
mountain mahogany - *Cercocarpus
   montanus*
narrowleaf cottonwood - *Populus
   augustifolia*
narrowleaf yucca - *Yucca angustissima*
netleaf oak - *Quercus reticulata*
New Mexico locust - *Robinia
   neomexicana*
one-seed juniper - *Juniperus
   monosperma*
osha - *Ligusticum porteri*
Palmer oak - *Quercus chrysolepis* var.
   palmeri or *Q. dunnii* or *Q. palmeri*
Palmer penstemon - *Penstemon palmeri*
penstemon - *Penstemon* spp.
phlox - *Phlox* spp.
pinyon pine - *Pinus edulis*
poison ivy - *Rhus radicans*
ponderosa pine - *Pinus ponderosa*
prickly pear - *Opuntia* spp.
purple nightshade - *Solanum xantii*
quaking aspen - *Populus tremuloides*
rabbitbrush - *Chrysothamnus* spp.
red osier dogwood - *Cornus stolonifera*
red willow - *Salix laevigata*
river sedge - *Carex* spp.
Rocky Mountain juniper - *Juniperus
   scopulorum*
sacred datura - *Datura meteloides*
scarlet gilia - *Ipomopsis aggregata*
scarlet sumac - *Rhus glabra*
senecio - *Senecio* spp.
shrub live oak - *Quercus turbinella*
silk-tassel bush - *Garrya* spp.
singleleaf ash - *Fraxinus anomala*
snakeweed - *Gutierrezia sarothrae*
spring beauty - *Claytonia lanceolata*
squawbush - *Rhus trilobata*
sugar sumac - *Rhus ovata*

sunflower - *Helianthus annuus*
tree-of-heaven - *Ailanthus altissima*
tumbleweed - *Salsola kali*
Utah juniper - *Juniperus osteosperma*
velvet ash - *Fraxinus pennsylvanica*
wallflower - *Erysimum* spp.
watercress - *Rorippa nasturtium-
   aquaticum*
wavyleaf oak - *Quercus undulata*
western soapberry - *Sapindus saponaria*
white fir - *Abies concolor*
white oak - *Quercus alba*
wild grape - *Vitis arizonica*
yellow monkeyflower - *Mimulus
   guttatus*

Animals
Abert's squirrel - *Sciurus aberti*
Abert's towhee - *Pipilo aberti*
acorn woodpecker - *Melanerpes for-
   micivorus*
American dipper - *Cinclus mexicanus*
American goldfinch - *Spinus tristis*
American kestrel - *Falco sparverius*
American robin - *Turdus migratorius*
Arctic grayling - *Thymallus arcticus*
Arizona gray squirrel - *Sciurus
   arizonensis*
Arizona treefrog - *Hyla wrightorum*
Arizona trout - *Salmo apache*
ash-throated flycatcher - *Myiarchus
   tyrannulus*
bald eagle - *Haliaeetus leucocephalus*
band-tailed pigeon - *Columba fasciata*
Bell's vireo - *Vireo bellii*
belted kingfisher - *Ceryle alcyon*
Bewick's wren - *Thryomanes bewickii*
bighorn sheep - *Ovis canadensis*
black catfish - *Ictalurus melas*
black-chinned hummingbird -
   Archilochus alexandri
black-crowned night heron - *Nycticorax
   nycticorax*
black-headed grosbeak - *Pheucticus
   melanocephalus*
black phoebe - *Sayornis nigricans*
black-throated gray warbler - *Dendroica
   nigrescens*

black-throated sparrow - *Amphispiza bilineata*
bluegill - *Lepomis macrochirus*
blue grosbeak - *Guiraca caerulea*
Brewer's blackbird - *Euphagus cyanocephalus*
Brewer's sparrow - *Spizella breweri*
bridled titmouse - *Parus wollweberi*
broad-tailed hummingbird - *Selasphorus platycercus*
brown creeper - *Certhia familiaris*
brown-crested flycatcher - *Myiarchus tyrannuius*
brown towhee - *Pipilo fuscus*
brown trout - *Salmo trutta*
bushtit - *Psaltriparus minimus*
caddis fly - Order Trichoptera
Canada goose - *Branta canadensis*
canyon wren - *Catherpes mexicanus*
carp - *Cyprinus carpio*
Cassin's kingbird - *Tyrannus vociferans*
cedar waxwing - *Bombycilla cedrorum*
channel catfish - *Ictalurus punctatus*
chipping sparrow - *Spizella passerina*
cinnamon teal - *Anas cyanoptera*
cliff chipmunk - *Eutamias dorsalis*
cliff swallow - *Hirundo pyrrhonota*
collared lizard - *Crotaphytus collaris*
Colorado River chub - *Gila robusta*
Colorado River squawfish - *Ptychocheilus lucius*
common black-hawk - *Buteogallus anthracinus*
common merganser - *Mergus merganser*
common nighthawk - *Chordeiles minor*
common yellowthroat - *Geothlypis trichas*
Cooper's hawk - *Accipiter cooperii*
Coues white-tailed deer - *Odocoileus virginianus* ssp. *couesi*
coyote - *Canis latrans*
crissal thrasher - *Toxostoma dorsale*
cutthroat trout - *Salmo clarki*
dark-eyed (gray-headed) junco - *Junco hyemalis*
desert-grassland whiptail - *Cnemidophorus uniparens*
eastern fence lizard - *Sceloporus undulatus*

fathead minnow - *Pimephales promelas*
flathead catfish - *Pilodictis olivaris*
Gambel's quail - *Callipepla gambelii*
Gila mountain-sucker - *Pantosteus clarki*
Gila sucker - *Catostomus insignis*
Gila trout - *Salmo gilae*
Gila woodpecker - *Melanerpes uropygialis*
golden-mantled ground squirrel - *Spermophilus lateralis*
Grace's warbler - *Dendroica graciae*
gray fox - *Urocyon cinereoargenteus*
gray-collared chipmunk - *Eutamias cinereicollis*
great blue heron - *Ardea herodias*
great horned owl - *Bubo virginianus*
great-tailed grackle - *Cassidix mexicanus*
green-backed heron - *Butorides striatus*
green sunfish - *Chaenobryttus cyanellus*
grizzly bear - *Ursus arctos*
hairy woodpecker - *Picoides villosus*
Harris' antelope squirrel - *Ammospermophilus harrisii*
hepatic tanager - *Piranga flava*
hermit thrush - *Catharus guttatus*
hooded oriole - *Icterus cucullatus*
house finch - *Carpodacus mexicanus*
house wren - *Troglodytes aedon*
killdeer - *Charadrius vociferus*
ladder-backed woodpecker - *Picoides scalaris*
largemouth bass - *Micropterus salmoides*
lazuli bunting - *Passerina amoena*
lesser goldfinch - *Carduelis psaltria*
Lincoln's sparrow - *Melospiza lincolnii*
loggerhead shrike - *Lanius ludovicianus*
Lucy's warbler - *Vermivora luciae*
mallard - *Anas platyrhynchos*
marsh wren - *Telmatodytes palustris*
Merriam's elk - *Cervus elaphus* ssp. *merriami*
mosquito fish - *Gambusia affinis*
mountain chickadee - *Parus gambeli*
mountain lion - *Felis concolor*
mourning dove - *Zenaida macroura*
mule deer - *Odocoileus hemionus*
narrow-headed gartersnake - *Thamnophis rufipunctatus*

northern cardinal - *Cardinalis cardinalis*
northern (red-shafted) flicker - *Colaptes auratus*
northern harrier - *Circus cyaneus*
northern mockingbird - *Mimus polyglottos*
northern (Bullock's) oriole - *Icterus galbula*
northern rough-winged swallow - *Stelgidopteryx ruficollis*
orange-crowned warbler - *Vermivora ruficapilla*
Page Springs snail - *Pyrgulopsis morrisoni*
painted redstart - *Myioborus pictus*
peregrine falcon - *Falco mexicanus*
phainopepla - *Phainopepla nitens*
pied-billed grebe - *Podilymbus podiceps*
pine siskin - *Carduelis pinus*
pinyon jay - *Gymnorhinus cyanocephalus*
plain titmouse - *Parus inornatus*
plateau whiptail - *Cnemidophorus velox*
pygmy nuthatch - *Sitta pygmaea*
rainbow trout - *Salmo gairdneri*
rattlesnake - *Crotalus* spp.
raven - *Corvus corax*
red-breasted nuthatch - *Sitta canadensis*
red-faced warbler - *Cardellina rubrifrons*
red shiner - *Notropis lutrensis*
red squirrel - *Tamiasciurus hudsonicus*
red-tailed hawk - *Buteo jamaicensis*
red-winged blackbird - *Agelaius phoeniceus*
ringtail cat - *Bassaricus astutus*
rockbass - *Ambloplites rupestris*
rock squirrel - *Spermophilus variegatus*
rock wren - *Salpinctes obsoletus*
ruby-crowned kinglet - *Regulus calendula*
rufous hummingbird - *Selasphorus rufus*
rufous-sided towhee - *Pipilo erythrophthalmus*
savannah sparrow - *Passerculus sandwichensis*
Say's phoebe - *Sayornis saya*
scrub jay - *Aphelocoma coerulescens*
sharp-shinned hawk - *Accipiter striatus*
short-horned lizard - *Phrynosoma douglassi*
side-blotched lizard - *Uta stansburiana*

solitary vireo - *Vireo solitarius*
song sparrow - *Melospiza melodia*
southwestern toad - *Bufo microscaphus*
spike dace - *Meda fulgida*
spotted owl - *Strix occidentalis*
spotted sandpiper - *Actitis macularia*
spotted skunk - *Spilogale gracilis*
striped skunk - *Mephitis mephitis*
smallmouth bass - *Micropterus dolomieui*
snowy egret - *Egretta thula*
spadefoot toad - *Scaphiopus hammondi*
speckled dace - *Rhinichthys osculus*
Steller's jay - *Cyanocitta stelleri*
summer tanager - *Piranga rubra*
Townsend's solitaire - *Myadestes townsendi*
tree lizard - *Urosaurus ornatus*
turkey vulture - *Cathartes aura*
verdin - *Auriparus flaviceps*
violet-green swallow - *Tachycineta thalassina*
Virginia's warbler - *Vermivora virginiae*
warbling vireo - *Vireo gilvus*
water pipit - *Anthus spinoletta*
western bluebird - *Sialia mexicana*
western kingbird - *Tyrannus verticalis*
western meadowlark - *Sturnella neglecta*
western wood pewee - *Contopus sordidulus*
western tanager - *Piranga ludoviciana*
white-breasted nuthatch - *Sitta carolinensis*
white-crowned sparrow - *Zonotrichia leucophrys*
white-throated swift - *Aeronautes saxatalis*
Wilson's warbler - *Wilsonia pusilla*
yellow-bellied sapsucker - *Sphyrapicus varius*
yellow-billed cuckoo - *Coccyzus americanus*
yellow-breasted chat - *Icteria virens*
yellow bullhead - *Ictalurus natalis*
yellow-headed blackbird - *Xanthocephalus xanthocephalus*
yellow-rumped (Audubon's) warbler - *Dendroica coronata*
yellow warbler - *Dendroica petechia*

□

A NATURAL HISTORY GLOSSARY

□

Alluvium—a general term for sediments laid down in river beds, flood plains, lakes, and fans at the foot of mountain slopes.

Basalt—an extrusive igneous, fine-grained, dark-colored rock.

Biome—a large geographic area named by the characteristic form of vegetation present.

Breccia—a rock made up of angular, coarse fragments.

Chaparral—a biome consisting of drought-tolerant, broad-leaved evergreen bushes, shrubs, or small trees occurring in more or less continuous stands.

Chert—extremely fine-grained varieties of silica such as flint and jasper.

Columnar jointing—basalt fractured into vertical columns upon cooling.

Colluvium—a general term for loose deposits of rock such as talus at the foot of a slope or cliff.

Community—an aggregate of organisms which form a distinct ecological unit; such a unit may be defined in terms of plants, animals, or both.

Crepuscular—animals that are active at dawn and dusk.

Crossbedding—the arrangement of thin layers of rock strata transverse or oblique to the main bedding planes, such as seen in the Coconino Sandstone.

Deciduous—plants that shed their leaves annually.

Disjunct species—an organism whose distribution is geographically scattered.

Diurnal—animals that are active during the day, as opposed to nocturnal.

Dog-tooth calcite—sharp-pointed crystals of calcium carbonate.

Ecology—the study of the relationship of plants and animals to each other and to their environment.

Ecotone—the area where two or more plant and/or animal communities intermingle.

Endemic species—an organism having a comparatively restricted distribution.

Erosion—the group of processes that loosen and remove rock material; includes weathering, solution, corrasion, and transportation.

Extrusive rocks—those igneous rocks derived from molten magma that has cooled above ground.

Fault—a fracture along which there has been displacement of the sides.

Habitat—a specific set of physical conditions that surrounds a species or community.

Igneous rocks—rocks formed from the solidification of molten rock (magma).

Intrusive rocks—igneous rocks derived from molten magma that has cooled beneath the surface of the ground.

Joint—a fracture in rock along which no appreciable movement has occurred.

Lava—molten rock that issues from a volcano or fissure in the earth's surface.

Limestone—a sedimentary rock composed predominantly of calcium carbonate.

Micro-habitat—the physical conditions surrounding an organism.

Mold—the fossil impression left in the surrounding rock by a shell or other organic structure.

Mudstone—a sedimentary rock composed of an indefinite mixture of clay, silt, and sand particles.

Relict species—an organism surviving in an environment that has undergone considerable change.

Parthenogenic reproduction—in vertebrate animals, reproduction without the combining of sperm with the egg.

Riparian—the bank of a river or pond.

Sandstone—a sedimentary rock composed predominantly of quartz grains.

Sedimentary rock—rock formed by the accumulation of sediment in water or from air (eolian deposits).

Shale—a sedimentary rock composed predominately of clay.

Silica—silicon dioxide; the mineral quartz.

Siltstone—a sedimentary rock composed predominantly of very fine-grained particles called silt.

Talus—collection of fallen rock debris which has formed a slope at the foot of a steeper cliff.

Volcanic bombs—occur when magma is shot into the air and cools into a bombshell-shape before hitting the ground.

Vesicular basalt—basalt that contains numerous small cavities due to the presence of gas bubbles as the basalt cooled.

Vug—a cavity often lined with a mineral different than the surrounding rock.

Weathering—the chemical action of air and rain water, and the mechanical action of changes in temperature that disintegrate rocks.

FURTHER READING

GENERAL

Abbey, Dawn, editor. *Dick Sutphen presents Sedona: Psychic Energy Vortexes*. Malibu, California: Valley of the Sun Publishing, 1986. Sedona has become noted among New Age believers as having four power spots where psychic energy flows from the earth: Boynton Canyon, Table Top Mountain, Cathedral Rock, and Bell Rock.

Aitchison, Stewart. *Oak Creek Canyon and the Red Rock Country of Arizona*. Sedona, Arizona: Bradshaw Color Studios, 1978. Sometimes out-of-print; contains checklists of vascular plants and vertebrate animals and detailed hiking trail descriptions. Some of the scientific information is outdated. May be found in libraries.

Arizona Highways, Volume 63, Number 3, 1987. Phoenix, Arizona. Contains several articles devoted to Oak Creek and vicinity. A number of older issues also contain articles about the area.

Grey, Zane. "Call of the Canyon", *The Ladies Home Journal*. Curtis Publishing Company, 1922, copyright renewed 1949 by Lina Elise Grey. A classic Western novel set in Oak Creek Canyon.

Hoffman, John F. *Sedona/Oak Creek Visual*. San Diego, California: Western Recreational Publications, 1987. A mostly pictorial treatment of the Oak Creek area.

Lee, Christopher Tom. *Secret Mountain/Red Canyon, Arizona: Resource and Management Alternatives*. Unpublished master's thesis, California State University, Fullerton, California, 1982. A study of the national park quality of the Oak Creek area.

"Oak Creek, Red Rock Country," *Plateau*, Volume 57, Number 1, 1986. Flagstaff, Arizona: Museum of Northern Arizona. A special issue by the Museum of Northern Arizona devoted to the natural history of the Oak Creek Canyon area.

"People of the Verde Valley," *Plateau*, Volume 53, Number 1, 1981. Flagstaff, Arizona: Museum of Northern Arizona. An entire issue devoted to the geology and human history of the Verde Valley.

Russell, Larry. *Arizona's Red Rock Country*. Flagstaff, Arizona: Northland Press, 1984. A lyrical description of the four seasons of Oak Creek Canyon accompanied by beautiful color photos.

Stegner, Wallace and Page Stegner. *American Places*. New York: E.P. Dutton, 1981. Contains an essay about Sedona's past and present.

BIOLOGY

Aitchison, Stewart. *Ecology of Oak Creek Canyon, Coconino County, Arizona*. Unpublished Phase 1 and 2 reports for Coconino National Forest, Flagstaff, Arizona, 1973. These two reports include inventories of the vascular, non-vascular plants, and vertebrates in the canyon and a human impact study at Cave Springs Campground.

Carothers, Steven W., R. Roy Johnson, and Stewart W. Aitchison. "Population Structure and Social Organization of Southwestern Riparian Birds." *American Zoologist*, Volume 14, 1974, pp. 97–108. This was a multi-year study of breeding birds along the Verde River, Dry Beaver Creek, and West Clear Creek.

"High Country Wildflowers." *Plateau*, Volume 58, Number 3, 1987. Flagstaff, Arizona: Museum of Northern Arizona. Entire issue devoted to the ecology of wildflowers.

Johnson, A.B. "The Bryophytes and Lichens of West Fork, Oak Creek Canyon." *Plateau*, Volume 36(2), 1963, pp. 54–62. If mosses and lichens are your interest, this is where to begin.

May, Eric. *An Examination of the Aquatic Insect Populations of Oak Creek, Arizona.* Unpublished master's thesis, Northern Arizona University, Flagstaff, Arizona, 1972.

McDougall, Walter B. *Seed Plants of Northern Arizona.* Flagstaff, Arizona: Museum of Northern Arizona, 1973. This is a technical plant key for identifying the seed plants of Northern Arizona.

Parrott, J.F. *A Seasonal Analysis of Aquatic Insect Populations in Oak Creek, Arizona.* Unpublished master's thesis, Northern Arizona University, Flagstaff, Arizona, 1975.

"Spring Wildflowers of Northern Arizona." *Plateau*, Volume 55, Number 3, 1984. Flagstaff, Arizona: Museum of Northern Arizona. A good introduction to the local flora.

Scott, Jan. *Seasonal Abundance and Distribution of Benthic Insects at Pumphouse Wash and Chavez Crossing in Oak Creek, Arizona.* Unpublished master's thesis, Northern Arizona University, Flagstaff, Arizona, 1982.

GEOLOGY

Blakey, Ronald C. "Pennsylvanian and Early Permian Paleogeography, Southern Colorado Plateau and Vicinity", *Paleozoic Paleogeography of West-Central United States*, 1980, pp. 234–257. T.D. Fouch, E.R. Magathan (eds.). Rocky Mountain Section, Society of Economic Paleontologists and Mineralogists. Information about the Schnebly Hill Formation.

Broomhall, Robert. *Geology of Dry Creek-West Fork Area, Central Arizona.* Unpublished master's thesis, Northern Arizona University, Flagstaff, Arizona, 1978.

Cloud, Robert. *Geology of the Munds Park-Oak Creek Canyon Area, Central Arizona.* Unpublished master's thesis, Northern Arizona University, Flagstaff, Arizona, 1983.

Elston, Donald P. "Rocks, Landforms, and Landscape Development in Central Arizona", *Landscapes of Arizona, The Geological Story*, 1984, pp. 151–173. T.L. Smiley, J.D. Nations, T.L. Pewe, J.P. Schafer (eds.). Lanham, Maryland: University Press of America.

Lucchita, Ivo. "Development of Landscape in Northwest Arizona: the Country of Plateaus and Canyons", *Landscapes of Arizona, The Geological Story*. T.L. Smiley, J.D. Nations, T.L. Pewe, J.P. Schafer (eds.). Lanham, Maryland: University Press of America, 1984.

Nations, Dale, J.C. Wilt and R.H. Hevly. "Cenozoic Paleogeography of Arizona", *Cenozoic Paleogeography of West- Central United States*, 1985, pp. 335–355. R.M. Flores, S.S. Kaplan (eds.). Rocky Mountain Section, Society of Economic Paleontologists and Mineralogists.

HIKING

McKelvey, M. and M. *Sedona and Red Rock Country Walking and Horseback Trail Map*. Sedona, Arizona, 1981. Topographic map showing many of the designated and unofficial routes in the area.

Sedona Westerners. *A Sampler of 108 Sedona Westerner Trail Walks*. Sedona, Arizona: Pronto Press, 1979. Reminiscences of memorable hikes in the Red Rock Country.

PREHISTORY

Fewkes, Jesse Walter. "Archeological Expedition to Arizona in 1895", *17th Annual Report of the Bureau of American Ethnology*. Washington, D.C., 1895-96. Fewkes was one of the first archaeologists to explore the Red Rock Country.

Fish, Paul R., Peter J. Pilles, Jr., and Suzanne K. Fish. "Colonies, Traders and Traits: The Hohokam in the North." *Current Issues in Hohokam Prehistory*. Arizona State University Anthropological Research Papers No. 23, Tempe, Arizona, 1980.

Hodge, Carle. *Ruins Along the River*. Tucson, Arizona: Southwest Parks and Monuments Association, 1986. Excellent summary of the area's prehistory for the lay-reader.

Khera, Sigrid and Patricia S. Mariella. "Yavapai." *Handbook of North American Indians*. Volume 10, 1983. Washington, D.C.: Smithsonian Institution. A summary of Yavapai history and culture.

Pilles, Jr., Peter J. "The Sinagua." *Exploration*. Annual Bulletin of the School of American Research, 1987. Latest ideas on the Sinagua culture.

"A Review of Yavapai Archaeology." *The Protohistoric Period in the North American Southwest, AD 1450-1700*. Arizona State University Anthropological Research Papers No. 24, Tempe, Arizona, 1981.

Shutler, Jr., Dick. "The Dry Creek Site: A Pre-pottery Lithic Horizon in the Verde Valley, Arizona." *Plateau*, Volume 23 (1), p. 10, 1950. Examines a site from the Archaic Period.

HISTORY

Cline, Platt. *They Came to the Mountain: The Story of Flagstaff*. Flagstaff, Arizona: Northern Arizona University and Northland Press, 1976. The definitive history of Flagstaff.

Hayden, Helen. *Village of Oak Creek*. Sedona, Arizona: Pronto Press, 1981.

Howard, William. *Sedona Reflections . . . Tales of Then for Now*. Sedona, Arizona: Pronto Press, 1981. Information on the life and times of John Jim Thompson and other early settlers.

McBride, Laura Purtymun. *Traveling by Tin Lizzie: The Great Model T Road Trip of 1924*. Sedona, Arizona: Pronto Press, 1980. Early travels around the country including Oak Creek; written by a Red Rock Country native.

Schroeder, Albert H. *Yavapai Indians: A Study of Yavapai History*. New York: Garland Publishing Co., 1974.

Sedona Westerners. *Those Early Days . . . Old-Timer's Memoirs—Oak Creek-Sedona and the Verde Valley Region of Northern Arizona*. Cottonwood, Arizona: The Verde Independent, 1975. The best oral history of the Red Rock Country.

Simmons, Isabel (ed.) *Cottonwood, Clarkdale, and Cornville History.* Cottonwood, Arizona: American Association of Retired Persons, Cottonwood Chapter 2021, 1975.

Shrub live oak

THE AUTHOR

Biologist-author Stewart Aitchison is a guide for Sven-Olof Lindblad's Special Expeditions, Inc. and escorts travelers on natural history trips through the southwestern United States.

His previously published books include *A Naturalist's San Juan River Guide*, *A Naturalist's Guide to Hiking the Grand Canyon*, *The Hiker's Guide to Arizona* (with Bruce Grubbs), and *Utah Wildlands*. He is a member of The Authors Guild, Inc. and the Society of Southwestern Authors. Aitchison makes his home in Flagstaff, Arizona.

NOTES

JoAnann

217 782 2035
782 7864
---
708 394-1713